Focus on Phonics - 3

by Gail V. Rice

Long Vowel Sounds

Student Workbook

Correlated to
Laubach Way to Reading
Skill Book 3

ISBN 0-88336-451-4

"EACH ONE TEACH ONE" ®

© 1982
New Readers Press
Publishing Division of Laubach Literacy International
Box 131, Syracuse, New York 13210

Printed in the United States of America

Designed by Kay Koschnick

Illustrated by Caris Lester and Chris Steenwerth

9 8 7 6 5 4 3 2

Practice 1: Short Vowels and Long Vowels

a   ā   e   ē   i   ī   o   ō   u   ū

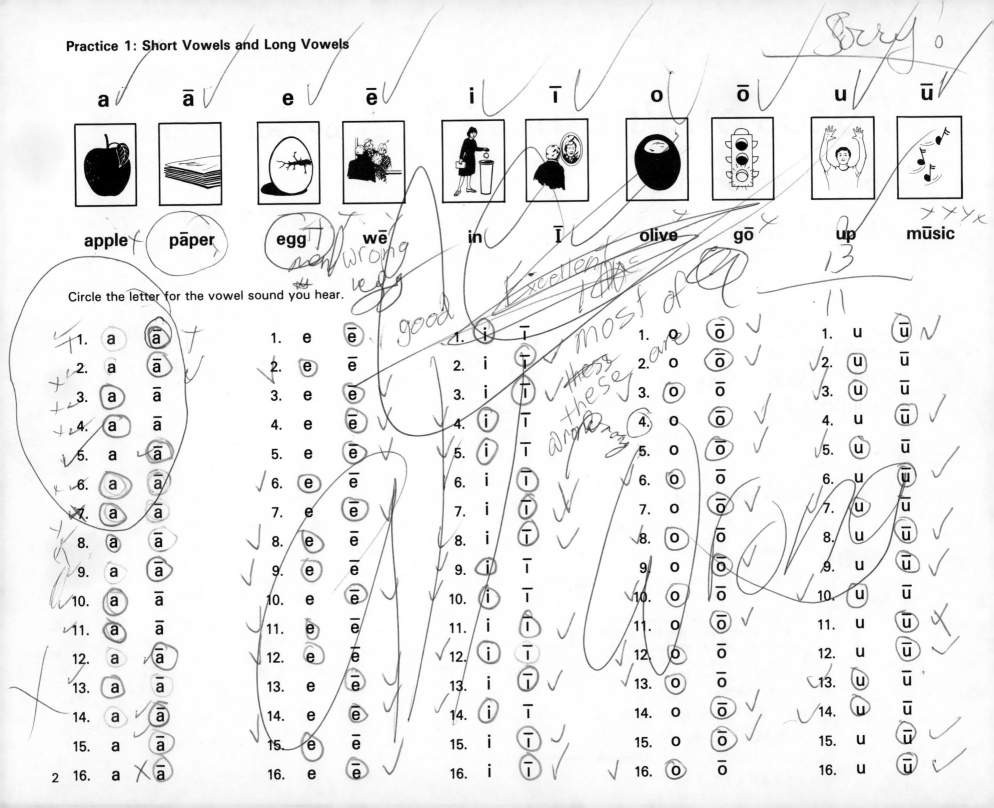

apple   pāper   egg   wē   in   ī   olive   gō   up   mūsic

Circle the letter for the vowel sound you hear.

	a	ā		e	ē		i	ī		o	ō		u	ū
1.	a	ā	1.	e	ē	1.	i	ī	1.	o	ō	1.	u	ū
2.	a	ā	2.	e	ē	2.	i	ī	2.	o	ō	2.	u	ū
3.	a	ā	3.	e	ē	3.	i	ī	3.	o	ō	3.	u	ū
4.	a	ā	4.	e	ē	4.	i	ī	4.	o	ō	4.	u	ū
5.	a	ā	5.	e	ē	5.	i	ī	5.	o	ō	5.	u	ū
6.	a	ā	6.	e	ē	6.	i	ī	6.	o	ō	6.	u	ū
7.	a	ā	7.	e	ē	7.	i	ī	7.	o	ō	7.	u	ū
8.	a	ā	8.	e	ē	8.	i	ī	8.	o	ō	8.	u	ū
9.	a	ā	9.	e	ē	9.	i	ī	9.	o	ō	9.	u	ū
10.	a	ā	10.	e	ē	10.	i	ī	10.	o	ō	10.	u	ū
11.	a	ā	11.	e	ē	11.	i	ī	11.	o	ō	11.	u	ū
12.	a	ā	12.	e	ē	12.	i	ī	12.	o	ō	12.	u	ū
13.	a	ā	13.	e	ē	13.	i	ī	13.	o	ō	13.	u	ū
14.	a	ā	14.	e	ē	14.	i	ī	14.	o	ō	14.	u	ū
15.	a	ā	15.	e	ē	15.	i	ī	15.	o	ō	15.	u	ū
16.	a	ā	16.	e	ē	16.	i	ī	16.	o	ō	16.	u	ū

2

Practice 2: Short a and Long ā

1

a   ā

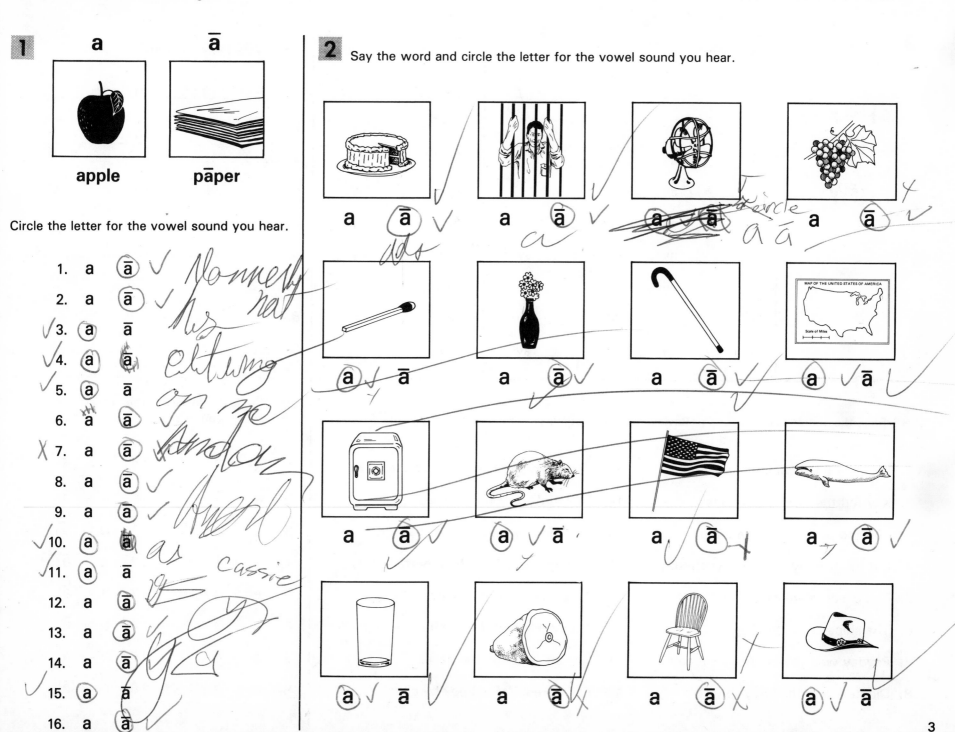

apple   pāper

Circle the letter for the vowel sound you hear.

1.   a   (ā)
2.   a   (ā)
3.   (a)   ā
4.   (a)   ā
5.   (a)   ā
6.   ā
7.   a   (ā)
8.   a   (ā)
9.   a   (ā)
10.   (a)   ā
11.   (a)   ā
12.   a   (ā)
13.   a   (ā)
14.   a   (ā)
15.   (a)   ā
16.   a   (ā)

2   Say the word and circle the letter for the vowel sound you hear.

a   (ā)   a   (ā)   a   (ā)   a   (ā)

(a)   ā   a   (ā)   a   (ā)   (a)   ā

a   (ā)   (a)   ā   a   (ā)   a   (ā)

(a)   ā   a   (ā)   a   (ā)   (a)   ā

3

Practice 3-A: Long a (-ay)

1

pay
day
-ay

2 Write the letters and say the word.

b	_____ ay	w	_____ ay
d	_____ ay		
g	_____ ay		
h	_____ ay		
l	_____ ay	F	_____ ay
m	_____ ay	J	_____ ay
p	_____ ay	K	_____ ay
r	_____ ay	M	_____ ay
s	_____ ay	R	_____ ay

3 Read the words.

hay	pay
say	Jay
way	lay
Ray	May
day	ray
Fay	bay
may	
gay	
Kay	

4 Write the word you hear.

1. _____   10. _____
2. _____   11. _____
3. _____   12. _____
4. _____   13. _____
5. _____   14. _____
6. _____   15. _____
7. _____
8. _____
9. _____

5 Read the sentences.   **Review words:** today, yesterday, payday, month

1. Jay may have something to say.
2. Kay fed the horses hay today.
3. This job pays fifty dollars a day.
4. Did the hen lay any eggs yesterday?
5. The children are happy and gay.
6. The ships are in the bay.
7. Payday was yesterday, not today.
8. Did he say which way to go?

9. Yesterday the farmer was pitching hay.
10. The sun's rays burned her.
11. Jay and Ray swam in the bay.
12. Mother's Day is in the month of May.
13. A car is coming this way.
14. Today the doctor will X-ray her leg.
15. Lay the letter on the desk.
16. Fay asked, "May I pay by check?"

6 Circle the letter for the vowel sound you hear.

1. a ā   9. a ā
2. a ā   10. a ā
3. a ā   11. a ā
4. a ā   12. a ā
5. a ā   13. a ā
6. a ā   14. a ā
7. a ā   15. a ā
8. a ā   16. a ā

Practice 3-B: Long a (-ay)

1

play

gray

-ay

2 Write the letters and say the word.

cl _____ ay   spr _____ ay

pl _____ ay

sl _____ ay

pr _____ ay

gr _____ ay

tr _____ ay

sw _____ ay

st _____ ay

str _____ ay

3 Read the words.

tray   sway

stay

pray

clay

gray

slay

stray

play

spray

4 Write the word you hear.

1. _____   10. _____

2. _____

3. _____

4. _____

5. _____

6. _____

7. _____

8. _____

9. _____

5 Read the sentences.   **New words:** maybe, always   **Review word:** away

1. Stack the dishes on the tray.

2. She sprays water on the plants.

3. Maybe I will stay for lunch.

4. Sister Ann is always praying.

5. Grandmother's hair is turning gray.

6. Kay is acting in the play.

7. Maybe that gray cat is a stray.

8. My kids always love to play with clay.

9. This bug spray keeps the ants away.

10. The bricks are made of clay.

11. God is never far away when I pray.

12. The trees sway in the wind.

13. Always stay away from stray pups.

14. Maybe she will play in the band.

15. Ray dropped the tray he was carrying.

16. Did the killer slay that man?

6 Circle the letter for the vowel sound you hear.

1. a   ā   9. a   ā

2. a   ā   10. a   ā

3. a   ā   11. a   ā

4. a   ā   12. a   ā

5. a   ā   13. a   ā

6. a   ā   14. a   ā

7. a   ā   15. a   ā

8. a   ā   16. a   ā

5

Practice 4A: Long a (-ail, -aim)

1

pail

nail

-ail

aim

claim

-aim

2 Write the letters and say the word.

b ____ ail	s ____ ail
f ____ ail	t ____ ail
h ____ ail	w ____ ail
j ____ ail	G ____ ail
m ____ ail	tr ____ ail
n ____ ail	sn ____ ail
p ____ ail	
qu ____ ail	____ aim
r ____ ail	cl ____ aim

3 Read the words.

rail	pail
nail	quail
Gail	fail
bail	snail
trail	hail
mail	tail
wail	
jail	claim
sail	aim

4 Write the word you hear.

1. _____   10. _____

2. _____   11. _____

3. _____   12. _____

4. _____   13. _____

5. _____   14. _____

6. _____   15. _____

7. _____   16. _____

8. _____   17. _____

9. _____

5 Read the sentences.   **New word:** hunter   **Review words:** baby, ever, never, Mason

1. Gail got a letter in the mail.

2. Kay is carrying a pail of water.

3. Two hunters are coming down the trail.

   The hunters are looking for quail.

4. Did that ship ever sail?

5. The pup wags his tail.

6. Gail hit the nail with a hammer.

7. Ray will bail him out of jail.

8. The sick baby let out a wail.

9. Mr. Mason held on to the rail.

10. She is clipping her nails.

11. Did Gail ever fail a test? No, never.

12. Put the snail in the fish tank.

13. The hunter aims his gun.

14. The hail is coming down hard.

15. Ed Mason claims that the land is his.

6 Circle the letter for the vowel sound you hear.

1. a	ā		9. a	ā
2. a	ā		10. a	ā
3. a	ā		11. a	ā
4. a	ā		12. a	ā
5. a	ā		13. a	ā
6. a	ā		14. a	ā
7. a	ā		15. a	ā
8. a	ā		16. a	ā

Practice 4B: Long a (-ain, -ait)

1

rain
chain
-ain

wait
-ait

2 Write the letters and say the word.

g _____ ain	gr _____ ain
l _____ ain	tr _____ ain
m _____ ain	st _____ ain
p _____ ain	Sp _____ ain
r _____ ain	spr _____ ain
ch _____ ain	str _____ ain
pl _____ ain	
br _____ ain	b _____ ait
dr _____ ain	w _____ ait

3 Read the words.

rain	strain
stain	lain
chain	grain
Spain	main
gain	drain
brain	train
pain	
sprain	wait
plain	bait

4 Write the word you hear.

1. _____   10. _____
2. _____   11. _____
3. _____   12. _____
4. _____   13. _____
5. _____   14. _____
6. _____   15. _____
7. _____   16. _____
8. _____   17. _____
9. _____

5 Read the sentences.   **New word:** nothing   **Review word:** lady

1. The farmer plants his grain.
2. Fish is the main dish.
3. Drain the water from the sink.
4. That runner is in training.
5. That pain killer acts on the brain.
6. We have nothing to gain by waiting.
7. Rain fell on the plains.
8. Wait for the fish to take the bait.

9. He has lain in bed for two days.
10. The lady is planning a trip to Spain.
11. Ed strained his back lifting the box.
12. He will bring you nothing but pain.
13. We waited in the rain for the train.
14. She twisted her arm and sprained it.
15. The lady chained the pup to the fence.
16. Nothing will get that stain out!

6 Circle the letter for the vowel sound you hear.

1. a ā   9. a ā
2. a ā   10. a ā
3. a ā   11. a ā
4. a ā   12. a ā
5. a ā   13. a ā
6. a ā   14. a ā
7. a ā   15. a ā
8. a ā   16. a ā

Practice 4-C: Long a (-aid, -aith, -aise, -aist, -aint)

1

paid   waist
-aid   -aist

faith   paint
-aith   -aint

raise
-aise

2 Write the letters and say the word.

	aid	r	____	aise
l	____	aid	pr	____	aise
m	____	aid			
p	____	aid	w	____	aist
r	____	aid			
br	____	aid			
			f	____	aint
			p	____	aint
f	____	aith	s	____	aint

3 Read the words.

raid	praise
maid	raise
aid	
braid	waist
laid	
paid	
	paint
	saint
faith	faint

4 Write the word you hear.

1. _____   10. _____
2. _____   11. _____
3. _____   12. _____
4. _____   13. _____
5. _____
6. _____
7. _____
8. _____
9. _____

5 Read the sentences.   **Review word:** paper

1. The hens laid many eggs.
2. The woman raised the flag.
3. We paid her to paint the kitchen.
4. Kay braids her little girl's hair.
5. This man has fainted.
   Can you give him first aid?
6. Our maid is asking for a raise.
7. I paid ten dollars for that painting.

8. He raised three children.
9. The cops will raid that bar.
10. Jay laid the paper on the desk.
11. Have faith! We will come to your aid.
12. The maid is making the beds.
13. Father always praises his children.
14. That saint had faith in God.
15. This skirt does not fit at the waist.

6 Circle the letter for the vowel sound you hear.

1. a ā   9. a ā
2. a ā   10. a ā
3. a ā   11. a ā
4. a ā   12. a ā
5. a ā   13. a ā
6. a ā   14. a ā
7. a ā   15. a ā
8. a ā   16. a ā

Practice 4-D: Long a (-air, -airy)

1

hair
chair
-air

hairy
dairy
-airy

2 Write the letters and say the word.

	air	d	_____	airy
f	_____ air	f	_____	airy
h	_____ air	h	_____	airy
p	_____ air			
ch	_____ air			
st	_____ air			

3 Read the words.

pair   hairy

stair   dairy

air   fairy

chair

fair

hair

4 Write the word you hear.

1. _____
2. _____
3. _____
4. _____
5. _____
6. _____
7. _____
8. _____
9. _____

5 Read the sentences.   **Review word:** table

1. Jan has blond hair.
2. Let in some fresh air.
3. He sells us a table and chairs.
4. That judge is a fair woman.
5. We get fresh milk from the dairy.
6. Pat is looking for a pair of socks.
7. Our baby son fell down the stairs.
8. Ray has a hairy chest.

9. Yesterday it was fair and hot.
10. Can you smell gas in the air?
11. He put on a pair of black pants.
12. The good fairy left me some money.
13. He carried the table up the stairs.
14. Jim sat back in his chair.
15. A can of hair spray is on the table.
16. The dairy farmers will go to the fair.

6 Circle the letter for the vowel sound you hear.

1. e $\bar{a}$	9. e $\bar{a}$
2. e $\bar{a}$	10. e $\bar{a}$
3. e $\bar{a}$	11. e $\bar{a}$
4. e $\bar{a}$	12. e $\bar{a}$
5. e $\bar{a}$	13. e $\bar{a}$
6. e $\bar{a}$	14. e $\bar{a}$
7. e $\bar{a}$	15. e $\bar{a}$
8. e $\bar{a}$	16. e $\bar{a}$

Practice 5-A: Long a (-ake)

1

take
cake
-ake

2 Write the letters and say the word.

b	_____ ake	J	_____ ake
c	_____ ake	sh	_____ ake
f	_____ ake	fl	_____ ake
l	_____ ake	br	_____ ake
m	_____ ake	st	_____ ake
r	_____ ake	sn	_____ ake
s	_____ ake		
t	_____ ake		
w	_____ ake		

3 Read the words.

take	brake
make	cake
flake	stake
bake	wake
rake	lake
Jake	sake
snake	
fake	
shake	

4 Write the word you hear.

1. _____   10. _____
2. _____   11. _____
3. _____   12. _____
4. _____   13. _____
5. _____   14. _____
6. _____   15. _____
7. _____
8. _____
9. _____

5 Read the sentences.   **New word:** mistake   **Review words:** I'll, radio, party

1. He shakes hands with his friend.
2. I'll bake cakes for the party.
3. It was a mistake to take that money.
4. My clock radio wakes me at six.
5. Jake is out fishing on the lake.
6. Dad bakes bread in the kitchen.
7. I had a big thick shake and some cake.
8. For your sake, do not make a mistake!

9. Jake takes the rake from the shed.
10. Do not wake up the baby.
11. We put up the tent with six stakes.
12. She makes money by taking pictures.
13. The paint is coming off in flakes.
14. There are many snakes by the lake.
15. He stepped on the brake by mistake.
16. That painting is a fake.

6 Circle the letter for the vowel sound you hear.

1. e ā   9. e ā
2. e ā   10. e ā
3. e ā   11. e ā
4. e ā   12. e ā
5. e ā   13. e ā
6. e ā   14. e ā
7. e ā   15. e ā
8. e ā   16. e ā

Practice 5-B: Long a (-ame, -ade)

1

name

came

-ame

made

shade

-ade

2 Write the letters and say the word.

c	_____ ame	f	_____ ade
f	_____ ame	m	_____ ade
g	_____ ame	w	_____ ade
s	_____ ame	sh	_____ ade
t	_____ ame	bl	_____ ade
sh	_____ ame	gr	_____ ade
bl	_____ ame	tr	_____ ade
fl	_____ ame	sp	_____ ade
fr	_____ ame		

3 Read the words.

tame	trade
shame	shade
flame	fade
same	spade
fame	made
blame	grade
came	wade
frame	blade
game	

4 Write the word you hear.

1. _____   10. _____

2. _____   11. _____

3. _____   12. _____

4. _____   13. _____

5. _____   14. _____

6. _____   15. _____

7. _____   16. _____

8. _____   17. _____

9. _____

5 Read the sentences.   **Review words:** name, Jason

1. Jason plans to trade in his car.

2. We came back the same way we went.

3. The colors are starting to fade.

4. Kay made a frame for the picture.

5. The first grade kids play games.

6. This blade is sharp. It cuts well.

7. The women have the same last name.

8. This bird is tame. It sits in my hand.

9. My son wades in the lake.

10. Do not blame me for what happens.

11. It is a shame his grades are so bad.

12. The building went up in flames.

13. Jason made a shade for our lamp.

14. The TV star wants fame and money.

15. He came out of the sun into the shade.

16. I bid one spade in the card game.

6 **Homonyms:** <u>made</u> and <u>maid</u>

The house was <u>made</u> of bricks.

She made six dollars an hour as a <u>maid</u>.

The <u>maid</u> cleans the hotel room.

Mom _____ a good dinner for us.

The _____ dusted the desk.

He _____ good money on that job.

A _____ lets the guests in.

11

Practice 5-C: Long a (-ate, -afe)

1

date

plate

-ate

safe

-afe

2 Write the letters and say the word.

	ate	cr	___	ate
d	___	ate	gr	___	ate
g	___	ate	sk	___	ate
h	___	ate	st	___	ate
l	___	ate			
m	___	ate			
r	___	ate	s	___	afe
K	___	ate			
pl	___	ate			

3 Read the words.

mate	Kate
ate	date
skate	gate
rate	crate
late	
state	
hate	safe
plate	
grate	

4 Write the word you hear.

1. _____   10. _____
2. _____   11. _____
3. _____   12. _____
4. _____   13. _____
5. _____   14. _____
6. _____
7. _____
8. _____
9. _____

5 Read the sentences.   **Review words:** April, I'll

1. Kate sells me a pair of skates.
2. What is the date? April first.
3. I'll shut the gate.
4. Our telephone rates went up in April.
5. Kate puts the money in the safe.
6. Pass me the plate of date-nut bread.
7. He hates to miss the state fair.
8. Birds mate late in the spring.

9. Our flag has a star for every state.
10. He slid to the plate. He was safe!
11. I hate to be late for a date.
12. Ray ate the eggs on his plate.
13. I'll send them a crate of apples.
14. It is not safe to skate there.
15. Jill grates an apple for a cake.
16. We ate a late dinner.

6 Circle the letter for the vowel sound you hear.

1. e ā   9. e ā
2. e ā   10. e ā
3. e ā   11. e ā
4. e ā   12. e ā
5. e ā   13. e ā
6. e ā   14. e ā
7. e ā   15. e ā
8. e ā   16. e ā

Practice 5-D: Long a (-ace, -ale)

1

face

place

-ace

pale

sale

-ale

2 Write the letters and say the word.

	ace	sp	_____ ace
f	_____ ace		
l	_____ ace	m	_____ ale
p	_____ ace	p	_____ ale
r	_____ ace	s	_____ ale
pl	_____ ace	t	_____ ale
br	_____ ace	wh	_____ ale
gr	_____ ace	sc	_____ ale
tr	_____ ace	st	_____ ale

3 Read the words.

lace	place
grace	
ace	tale
brace	scale
race	pale
pace	sale
trace	male
face	whale
space	stale

4 Write the word you hear.

1. _____ 10. _____

2. _____ 11. _____

3. _____ 12. _____

4. _____ 13. _____

5. _____ 14. _____

6. _____ 15. _____

7. _____ 16. _____

8. _____ 17. _____

9. _____

5 Read the sentences. **New words:** Grace, Dale **Review word:** paper

1. This bread is stale. Is it on sale?

2. Grace stands on the scales.

3. Dale's face looks very pale.

4. Put paper over the map and trace it.

5. The brace held his neck in place.

6. We raced to put a man in space.

7. Grace laid down the ace of spades.

8. A whale looks like a big fish.

9. Mom tells the children fairy tales.

10. Dale says grace at the dinner table.

11. The pet shop has a male cat for sale.

12. This place has lots of parking space.

13. The horse is running at a fast pace.

 He may take first place in the race.

14. Dale is a male nurse.

15. Grace trims the dress with lace.

6 Homonyms: <u>sale</u> and <u>sail</u>

She buys dresses on <u>sale</u>.

They <u>sail</u> the boat across the lake.

The shop has a _____ on hats.

That car is not for _____ .

When does the ship _____ ?

The wind catches the _____ .

1

gave

shave

-ave

tape

grape

-ape

2 Write the letters and say the word.

c	_____ ave		_____ ape
g	_____ ave	c	_____ ape
p	_____ ave	r	_____ ape
s	_____ ave	t	_____ ape
w	_____ ave	sh	_____ ape
sh	_____ ave	dr	_____ ape
sl	_____ ave	gr	_____ ape
br	_____ ave	scr	_____ ape
gr	_____ ave		

3 Read the words.

save	rape
wave	cape
grave	drape
slave	ape
cave	tape
gave	scrape
brave	grape
shave	shape
pave	

4 Write the word you hear.

1. _____   10. _____

2. _____   11. _____

3. _____   12. _____

4. _____   13. _____

5. _____   14. _____

6. _____   15. _____

7. _____   16. _____

8. _____   17. _____

9. _____

5 Read the sentences.   **New words:** Dave, escape   **Review words:** paper, jungle, where

1. Kate saves me a jar of grape jelly.

2. They will pave that street.

3. Dave gave Ann a fur cape.

4. Scrape the plates and stack them.

5. The ship sailed on the waves.

6. He plays the tape I gave him.

7. The brave slaves wanted to escape.

8. The kids hid in a dark cave.

9. Dave shaves his face every day.

10. This tape will stick to the paper.

11. Did he rape her? No, she escaped.

12. Kay waves to her friend Dave.

13. A brave cop saved us from harm.

14. The red drapes are in good shape.

15. No one can escape the grave.

16. Where do apes live? In the jungle.

6 Homonyms: <u>male</u> and <u>mail</u>

Is that dog a <u>male</u> or female?

We got a package in the <u>mail</u>.

_____ this card for me.

That cat is a _____ .

Two letters came in the _____ .

Ed is a _____ nurse.

Practice 5-F: Long a (-age, -ane, -ange)

1

page

-age

plane

-ane

change

-ange

2 Write the letters and say the word.

_____ age   c _____ ane

c _____ age   l _____ ane

p _____ age   m _____ ane

r _____ age   pl _____ ane

w _____ age   cr _____ ane

st _____ age

r _____ ange

ch _____ ange

str _____ ange

3 Read the words.

page   mane

wage   cane

age   crane

stage   plane

rage   lane

cage

change

strange

range

4 Write the word you hear.

1. _____   10. _____

2. _____   11. _____

3. _____   12. _____

4. _____   13. _____

5. _____   14. _____

6. _____

7. _____

8. _____

9. _____

5 Read the sentences.   **New words:** danger, stranger   **Review word:** Jane

1. Jane never tells her age.

2. Look at the strange bird in the cage.

3. Do you have change for a dollar?

4. Jane has a gas range in her kitchen.

5. Stay out of danger.

6. Grandmother carries a cane.

7. The plane was in danger of crashing.

8. Dave lifts the boxes with a crane.

9. I met a stranger on the plane.

10. Kate brushes the horse's mane.

11. Jane wants to act on the stage.

12. The car changes lanes.

13. A cop's job has many dangers.

But it pays good wages.

14. The stranger went into a mad rage.

15. Turn to page two.

6 Homonyms: <u>plane</u> and <u>plain</u>

The <u>plane</u> flew over the plains.

I like fancy clothes, not <u>plain</u> ones.

She has on a _____ red dress.

The _____ is taking off.

That land is a flat _____ .

She made it _____ that she was

mad at us.

Practice 5-G: Long **a** (-ase, -aste, -aze, -azy)

1

case	gaze
vase	**-aze**
-ase	
taste	lazy
waste	**-azy**
-aste	

2 Write the letters and say the word.

b _____ ase   d _____ aze

c _____ ase   g _____ aze

v _____ ase   h _____ aze

ch _____ ase   bl _____ aze

                   gl _____ aze

h _____ aste   gr _____ aze

p _____ aste

t _____ aste   l _____ azy

w _____ aste   cr _____ azy

3 Read the words.

vase	haze
chase	glaze
case	daze
base	graze
	blaze
paste	gaze
waste	
haste	crazy
taste	lazy

4 Write the word you hear.

1. _____   10. _____

2. _____   11. _____

3. _____   12. _____

4. _____   13. _____

5. _____   14. _____

6. _____   15. _____

7. _____   16. _____

8. _____

9. _____

5 Read the sentences.   **Review word:** David

1. David's pup chases cats.

2. This cake tastes good.

3. The lazy horses graze on the hill.

4. The runner ran to first base.

5. That vase is a waste of money!

6. Haste makes waste.

7. That crazy man is in a daze.

   He just gazes into space.

8. David put out the blaze with water.

9. The cop chased the man up the street.

10. She glazed the ham with jelly.

11. That store sells pop by the case.

12. The paste sticks to my fingers.

13. The mist made a haze in the air.

14. We have other plans in case it rains.

15. The lazy man says I am crazy to work.

6 Homonyms: <u>waste</u> and <u>waist</u>

That movie was a <u>waste</u> of time.

He tightens the belt around his <u>waist</u>.

The pants fit well at the _____ .

Put the trash in the _____ can.

Save money. Do not _____ it.

Take in the dress at the _____ .

Practice 5-H: Long a (-are, -ary)

1

care

share

-are

Mary

scary

-ary

2 Write the letters and say the word.

b ____ are	sp ____ are
c ____ are	st ____ are
d ____ are	sc ____ are
f ____ are	squ ____ are
m ____ are	
r ____ are	v ____ ary
sh ____ are	M ____ ary
fl ____ are	G ____ ary
gl ____ are	sc ____ ary

3 Read the words.

mare	care
stare	glare
fare	share
rare	scare
spare	
bare	Gary
flare	vary
square	scary
dare	Mary

4 Write the word you hear.

1. _____   10. _____
2. _____   11. _____
3. _____   12. _____
4. _____   13. _____
5. _____   14. _____
6. _____   15. _____
7. _____   16. _____
8. _____   17. _____
9. _____

5 Read the sentences.   **New word:** parent   **Review words:** marry, carry, very

1. I share my cares and worries with him.
2. The way he stares at us scares me.
3. Pork must never be served rare.
4. Parents take care of their children.
5. That mare is the best horse we have.
6. Gary was too scared to take the dare.
7. Bus fares vary from place to place.
8. Gary's parents want him to marry Kay.

9. Mary stares at the rare stamps.
10. I share my money with my parents.
11. The cop lit a flare.
12. They do not care for square dances.
13. In case of a flat, I carry a spare.
14. The hot pot burned my bare hands.
15. I watched a very scary picture on TV.
16. The drapes keep out the sun's glare.

6 **Homonyms:** fare and fair

The bus fare went up. It isn't fair!

Will the weather be cloudy or fair?

Mark the papers good, fair, or poor.

Today will be _____ and hot.

The bus _____ is fifty cents.

His work is just _____ .

She sells jam at the _____ .

17

Practice 6: Review of Long **a**

1 Look at the picture and say the word. Then write the word.

_____ _____ _____ _____ _____ _____

---

2 Circle all the words that are the same as the first one.

pail	pal	(bail)	(pale)	(pail)	leap	(pail)	(paid)
late	(date)	(late)	tale	(plate)	(late)	(hate)	lute
wage	(wage)	wedge	wag	(wade)	(wage)	(age)	(rage)
paste	past	(baste)	(paste)	pest	peat	(taste)	(paste)

3 Make at least **10** words with these beginnings and endings.

l	ake
st	ay
m	aid
br	ain

_____ _____ _____

_____ _____ _____

_____ _____ _____

_____ _____ _____

4 Use these words to fill in the blanks:

rain   taste   care   tray
paint   game   fail   face

1. Did Dave pass the test or _fail_ it?

2. She laid the plates on the _tray_.

3. The farmers are praying for _rain_.

4. We came to the _game_ to see him play.

5. Did you _taste_ the cake Jane baked?

6. Kay's _face_ was pale, but she did not faint.

7. Mary does not _care_ about saving money.

8. I may _paint_ the chair red.

Practice 7-A: Long e (-e, -ee)

1

we

he

-e

see

tree

-ee

2 Write the letters and say the word.

b _____ e   b _____ ee

h _____ e   f _____ ee

m _____ e   s _____ ee

w _____ e   t _____ ee

sh _____ e   fl _____ ee

                                  fr _____ ee

                                   tr _____ ee

                                 thr _____ ee

                                 spr _____ ee

3 Read the words.

we	tree
be	fee
she	see
me	three
he	bee
	flee
	spree
	tee
	free

4 Write the word you hear.

1. _____   10. _____

2. _____   11. _____

3. _____   12. _____

4. _____   13. _____

5. _____   14. _____

6. _____

7. _____

8. _____

9. _____

5 Read the sentences.   **New words:** Dee, agree   **Review words:** it's, didn't, coffee, cost, Lee

1. Lee planted three trees.

2. Did she agree to pay the fee?

3. The bee didn't sting me.

4. Dee gave me a golf tee.

5. The cost of coffee will be going up.

6. Do we agree on what picture to see?

7. There is no fee. It's free.

8. Lee went on a spending spree.

9. It's plain to see he is worried.

10. Dee will be free at three o'clock.

11. Let me see what it costs.

12. The bees have a nest in that tree.

13. Dee's son will be three in May.

14. She drank three cups of coffee.

15. If you set him free, he will flee.

16. We didn't agree with Lee.

6 Circle the letter for the vowel sound you hear.

1. e   ē   9. e   ē

2. e   ē   10. e   ē

3. e   ē   11. e   ē

4. e   ē   12. e   ē

5. e   ē   13. e   ē

6. e   ē   14. e   ē

7. e   ē   15. e   ē

8. e   ē   16. e   ē

Practice 7-B: Long e (-eed, -eef, -eem)

1

need
feed
-eed

beef
-eef

seem
-eem

2 Write the letters and say the word.

d _____ eed   tw _____ eed

f _____ eed

n _____ eed

s _____ eed

w _____ eed

bl _____ eed   b _____ eef

br _____ eed

fr _____ eed

sp _____ eed   s _____ eem

3 Read the words.

bleed   weed

need

speed

freed

seed

tweed   beef

feed

breed

deed   seem

4 Write the word you hear.

1. _____   10. _____

2. _____   11. _____

3. _____   12. _____

4. _____

5. _____

6. _____

7. _____

8. _____

9. _____

5 Read the sentences.   **New word:** greedy   **Review words:** cost, eleven, ever, it's, sandwich

1. The cops stopped him for speeding.

2. The greedy man wants a bigger share.

3. Dee cut her hand. It's bleeding.

4. We need one bag of grass seed.

5. It seems the cost of beef is going up.

6. It's eleven. I need to feed the baby.

7. Weed the garden; then plant the seeds.

8. The king was greedy for land.

9. She feeds us hot beef sandwiches.

10. Do you ever do good deeds?

11. We need to speed things up.

12. My tweed slacks cost eleven dollars.

13. Lee seems to be a very greedy man.

14. That is a rare breed of dog.

15. The slaves were freed in 1863.

16. This deed says the house is his.

6 Circle the letter for the vowel sound you hear.

1. e ē   9. e ē

2. e ē   10. e ē

3. e ē   11. e ē

4. e ē   12. e ē

5. e ē   13. e ē

6. e ē   14. e ē

7. e ē   15. e ē

8. e ē   16. e ē

Practice 7-C: Long e (-eek, -eel, -een)

1

week
peek
-eek

feel
wheel
-eel

green
-een

2 Write the letters and say the word.

p _____ eek   r _____ eel

s _____ eek   wh _____ eel

w _____ eek   st _____ eel

ch _____ eek

cr _____ eek   s _____ een

                     t _____ een

f _____ eel   qu _____ een

h _____ eel   gr _____ een

p _____ eel   scr _____ een

3 Read the words.

week   wheel

peek   peel

creek   feel

seek

cheek   queen

            seen

reel   green

heel   screen

steel   teen

4 Write the word you hear.

1. _____   10. _____

2. _____   11. _____

3. _____   12. _____

4. _____   13. _____

5. _____   14. _____

6. _____   15. _____

7. _____   16. _____

8. _____

9. _____

5 Read the sentences.   **New word:** between   **Review words:** Green, eight, eighteen, where

1. A screen keeps the bugs out.

2. I have not seen her for eight weeks.

3. Lee's cheeks are red. He feels hot.

4. There are bad feelings between us.

5. A wheel fell off the little green car.

6. He is seeking work at the steel mill.

7. Take a peek at the gift in this box.

8. In another week, Dee will be eighteen.

9. Where is the queen?

   She marches between the two kings.

10. I feel like fishing at the creek.

    I need my rod and reel.

11. Peel an apple, and chop it up.

12. Jason Green is in his teens.

    He is between the ages of 13 and 19.

13. The heels are worn down.

6 Circle the letter for the vowel sound you hear.

1. i ē   9. i ē

2. i ē   10. i ē

3. i ē   11. i ē

4. i ē   12. i ē

5. i ē   13. i ē

6. i ē   14. i ē

7. i ē   15. i ē

8. i ē   16. i ē

Practice 7-D: Long e (-eet, -eer)

1

meet

feet

-eet

beer

cheer

-eer

2 Write the letters and say the word.

b	_____ eet	b	_____ eer
f	_____ eet	d	_____ eer
m	_____ eet	p	_____ eer
sh	_____ eet	qu	_____ eer
fl	_____ eet	ch	_____ eer
gr	_____ eet	st	_____ eer
sl	_____ eet	sn	_____ eer
sw	_____ eet		
str	_____ eet		

3 Read the words.

meet	cheer
sleet	peer
feet	sneer
sweet	deer
fleet	steer
beet	beer
street	queer
sheet	
greet	

4 Write the word you hear.

1. _____ 10. _____

2. _____ 11. _____

3. _____ 12. _____

4. _____ 13. _____

5. _____ 14. _____

6. _____ 15. _____

7. _____ 16. _____

8. _____

9. _____

5 Read the sentences.   **Review words:** potatoes, fifteen

1. Beef comes from steers.

2. She greets every person she meets.

3. Tuck the sheets in.

4. We canned beets and sweet potatoes.

5. Rain and sleet made the street slick.

6. The robber sneered at the cop.

7. After I ran the race, my feet hurt.

8. A fleet of ships sailed into the bay.

9. They greeted us with cheers.

10. Meet me at the shop down the street.

11. We ate potato chips and drank beer.

12. Dee can steer that big truck.

13. She has a queer look on her face.

14. The deer was standing fifteen feet away.

15. I like my coffee sweet.

16. Lee peered at the sheet of paper.

6 Circle the letter for the vowel sound you hear.

1. i ē   9. i ē

2. i ē   10. i ē

3. i ē   11. i ē

4. i ē   12. i ē

5. i ē   13. i ē

6. i ē   14. i ē

7. i ē   15. i ē

8. i ē   16. i ē

Practice 7-E: Long e (-eep, -eech, -eeth)

1

keep
sleep
-eep

speech
-eech

teeth
-eeth

2 Write the letters and say the word.

d	_____ eep	st	_____ eep
j	_____ eep	sw	_____ eep
k	_____ eep		
p	_____ eep	b	_____ eech
w	_____ eep	l	_____ eech
sh	_____ eep	sp	_____ eech
ch	_____ eep	scr	_____ eech
cr	_____ eep		
sl	_____ eep	t	_____ eeth

3 Read the words.

sheep	weep
keep	jeep
sweep	
peep	speech
deep	beech
steep	screech
creep	leech
sleep	
cheep	teeth

4 Write the word you hear.

1. _____   10. _____
2. _____   11. _____
3. _____   12. _____
4. _____   13. _____
5. _____   14. _____
6. _____   15. _____
7. _____   16. _____
8. _____
9. _____

5 Read the sentences.   **New word:** blood   **Review word:** didn't

1. This fence keeps the sheep in.
2. Our baby is learning to creep.
3. Sweep up this dirt.
4. Dee fell into a deep sleep.
5. The nurse keeps checking his blood.
6. Lee didn't brush his teeth.
7. Her speech made me weep.
8. He parked the jeep on a steep hill.

9. The cut was deep. Blood gushed out.
10. His speech put me to sleep.
11. We get nuts from beech trees.
12. Ed didn't want to keep his jeep.
13. A leech is a worm that sucks blood.
14. The birds are peeping and cheeping.
15. The baby's teeth were hurting him.
    He let out a screech.

6 Circle the letter for the vowel sound you hear.

1. i ē   9. i ē
2. i ē   10. i ē
3. i ē   11. i ē
4. i ē   12. i ē
5. i ē   13. i ē
6. i ē   14. i ē
7. i ē   15. i ē
8. i ē   16. i ē

1

tea

-ea

read

-ead

speak

-eak

2 Write the letters and say the word.

p	_____ ea	b	_____ eak
s	_____ ea	l	_____ eak
t	_____ ea	p	_____ eak
fl	_____ ea	w	_____ eak
		cr	_____ eak
b	_____ ead	sn	_____ eak
l	_____ ead	sp	_____ eak
r	_____ ead	str	_____ eak
pl	_____ ead	squ	_____ eak

3 Read the words.

sea	peak
flea	sneak
pea	weak
tea	speak
	leak
lead	squeak
bead	beak
plead	creak
read	streak

4 Write the word you hear.

1. _____	10. _____
2. _____	11. _____
3. _____	12. _____
4. _____	13. _____
5. _____	14. _____
6. _____	15. _____
7. _____	16. _____
8. _____	17. _____
9. _____	

5 Read the sentences.   **New word:** its   **Review words:** traffic, water

1. We planted green peas in the garden.

2. This tea is very weak.

3. The pup scratches its fleas.

4. Lead us up to the peak.

5. He is so weak he cannot speak.

6. That rocking chair squeaks.

7. She agreed to plead my case.

8. David leads his class in reading.

9. Water is dripping. Fix the leak.

10. The stairs creak as he sneaks up.

11. He gave her a string of beads.

12. Her hair has streaks of gray.

13. Traffic is at its peak at eight.

14. She loves to read about the sea.

15. Dee will speak at the tea.

16. The bird pecks with its sharp beak.

6 Homonyms: <u>weak</u> and <u>week</u>

The <u>weak</u> man is getting stronger.

He went on vacation for a <u>week</u>.

The sick man was very _____ .

There are seven days in a _____ .

They will visit us for one _____ .

The legs on that chair are _____ .

Practice 8-B: Long e (-eam, -eat)

1

team
dream
-eam

eat
meat
-eat

2 Write the letters and say the word.

b	_____ eam			eat
s	_____ eam	b	_____ eat
t	_____ eam	h	_____ eat
gl	_____ eam	m	_____ eat
cr	_____ eam	n	_____ eat
dr	_____ eam	s	_____ eat
st	_____ eam	ch	_____ eat
str	_____ eam	wh	_____ eat
scr	_____ eam		

3 Read the words.

steam	neat
cream	beat
beam	wheat
dream	heat
seam	eat
gleam	cheat
scream	meat
stream	seat
team	

4 Write the word you hear.

1. _____   10. _____
2. _____   11. _____
3. _____   12. _____
4. _____   13. _____
5. _____   14. _____
6. _____   15. _____
7. _____   16. _____
8. _____   17. _____
9. _____

5 Read the sentences.   **Review words:** people, eaten, ever

1. I keep my apartment neat.

2. She always eats wheat bread.

3. We dream of beating the other team.

4. Has she ever cheated on a test?

5. Lee likes cream in his coffee.

6. The new car is gleaming in the sun.

7. The bad dream made him scream.

8. Ask the people to be seated.

9. She heats the meat by steaming it.

10. "Our team is winning!" he screams.

11. That seam is ripped. Stitch it up.

12. He has never eaten any meat.

13. Beat the eggs. Then add cream.

14. His writing is not very neat.

15. Many people fish at that stream.

16. A large beam fell in the barn.

6 **Homonyms:** <u>meat</u> and <u>meet</u>

Roast this <u>meat</u> for two hours.

We are pleased to <u>meet</u> you.

Let's <u>meet</u> at noon today.

We will _____ there for lunch.

Heat the _____ in a big pot.

Did you _____ my sister?

Beef is the _____ I like.

Practice 8-C: Long e (-eal, -ean, -eaf)

1

meal
steal
-eal
bean
clean
-ean
leaf
-eaf

2 Write the letters and say the word.

d _____ eal	b _____ ean
h _____ eal	l _____ ean
m _____ eal	m _____ ean
r _____ eal	D _____ ean
s _____ eal	J _____ ean
v _____ eal	j _____ eans
st _____ eal	cl _____ ean
squ _____ eal	
	l _____ eaf

3 Read the words.

real	Jean
heal	mean
seal	clean
meal	Dean
steal	lean
deal	bean
squeal	jeans
veal	
	leaf

4 Write the word you hear.

1. _____   10. _____
2. _____   11. _____
3. _____   12. _____
4. _____   13. _____
5. _____   14. _____
6. _____   15. _____
7. _____   16. _____
8. _____
9. _____

5 Read the sentences.   **New word:** really   **Review words:** water, wasn't, again

1. The cut healed, but it left a scar.

2. I got a really good deal on that car.

3. A leaf dropped off the tree.

4. The brakes squeal as the car stops.

5. We had veal and green beans to eat.

   Dean cleaned up after the meal.

6. Jean sealed the letter.

7. It was mean to steal that money.

8. The meal wasn't really good.

9. Jean really means what she says.

10. She put on a clean pair of jeans.

11. The seal is swimming in the water.

12. That painting is fake, not real.

13. Dean wasn't stealing again, was he?

14. Jean likes lean meat.

15. Deal the cards again.

6 Homonyms: <u>heal</u> and <u>heel</u>

His wounds did not <u>heal</u>.

Repair the <u>heels</u> on these shoes.

Measure her foot from <u>heel</u> to toe.

That cut will _____ quickly.

This _____ fell off. Fix it.

Doctors want to _____ people.

He dug his _____s into the sand.

26

Practice 8-D: Long e (-each, -eash, -east, -eap)

1

each   east
teach   least
-each   **-east**

leash   cheap
-eash   **-eap**

2 Write the letters and say the word.

each   east
b _____ each   b _____ east
p _____ each   f _____ east
r _____ each   l _____ east
t _____ each   y _____ east
bl _____ each
pr _____ each h _____ eap
           l _____ eap
l _____ eash ch _____ eap

3 Read the words.

reach   least
peach   beast
bleach   east
each   yeast
preach   feast
teach
beach   leap
       cheap
leash   heap

4 Write the word you hear.

1. _____ 10. _____
2. _____ 11. _____
3. _____ 12. _____
4. _____ 13. _____
5. _____ 14. _____
6. _____ 15. _____
7. _____ 16. _____
8. _____
9. _____

5 Read the sentences.   **Review words:** teacher

1. Jean leaped to her feet.

2. We hunted for shells on the beach.

3. Go east until you reach First Street.

4. Dinner was a real feast! We had veal.

   I fixed green beans and yeast bread.

   Then we had peaches and cream.

5. Jean led the pup on a leash.

6. Father Dean loves to preach and teach.

7. Add at least one cup of bleach.

8. This car costs the least. It's cheap.

9. The teacher helps each one of us.

10. Lee reached for a box of bleach.

11. A heap of papers lay on the desk.

12. Peaches are cheap this summer.

13. Can he tame that beast?

14. Each of us will teach a class.

6 **Homonyms:** steal and steel

The thief steals her jewels.

The runner steals a base.

Steel is stronger than iron.

Did he _____ your TV set?

Robbers want to _____ her purse.

The building has _____ beams.

That car is made of _____ .

Practice 8-E: Long e (-ear, -eard)

1

dear

year

-ear

beard

-eard

2 Write the letters and say the word.

	ear	sh	_____	ear(s)
d	_____ ear	cl	_____	ear
f	_____ ear	sp	_____	ear
g	_____ ear	sm	_____	ear
h	_____ ear			
n	_____ ear			
r	_____ ear			
t	_____ ear			
y	_____ ear	b	_____	eard

3 Read the words.

tear	smear
near	gear
fear	shear
ear	year
clear	
dear	
spear	
rear	
hear	beard

4 Write the word you hear.

1. _____   10. _____

2. _____   11. _____

3. _____   12. _____

4. _____   13. _____

5. _____   14. _____

6. _____

7. _____

8. _____

9. _____

5 Read the sentences.   **New words:** nearly, clearly

1. Tears ran down her cheeks.

2. He made it clear that I must not go.

3. His ears are bad. He cannot hear well.

   Stand near him and speak clearly.

4. Trim your beard with a pair of shears.

5. Her hand is near the gearshift.

6. She was a dear friend for many years.

7. Take your camping gear on the trip.

8. She picked nearly fifty ears of corn.

9. The ink on that paper is smeared.

10. Lee sees clearly with his glasses on.

11. We sat in the rear of the bus.

12. Each year farmers shear their sheep.

13. The man speared a fish.

14. I fear we are about to hear bad news.

   My mother is nearly in tears.

6 **Homonyms:** <u>beat</u> and <u>beet</u>

Farmers grow <u>beets</u>.

That runner <u>beat</u> me!

That music has a good <u>beat</u>.

He <u>beat</u> the animals with a stick.

_____ the eggs.

This _____ is from my garden.

She _____ me in the race.

I _____ on the drum.

Practice 9-A: Long e (-ey, -e – e)

1

key

money

-ey

Pete

these

-e-e

2 Write the letters and say the word.

-ey

k _____ ey

hock _____ ey

turk _____ ey

vall _____ ey

mon _____ ey

hon _____ ey

-e-e

h _____ ere

th _____ ese

P _____ ete

_____ Eve

St _____ eve

3 Read the words.

valley	Pete
hockey	these
money	Eve
key	here
turkey	Steve
honey	

4 Write the word you hear.

1. _____   10. _____

2. _____   11. _____

3. _____

4. _____

5. _____

6. _____

7. _____

8. _____

9. _____

5 Read the sentences.   **New word:** even   **Review words:** evening, more, repair, again

1. These car keys are hers.

2. Pete and Eve went to a hockey game.

3. Ed makes even more money than Lee.

4. He is planning a New Year's Eve party.

5. Steve plans to sell these turkeys.

6. Can Eve repair these clocks?

7. Here is the key for that lock.

8. Ed and I got even shares of the money.

9. We had a turkey dinner this evening.

10. Pete keeps the car at an even speed.

11. There are honey bees in the valley.

12. Shop here. Get more for less money.

13. Repairs cost a lot of money.

14. Steve's hockey team beat ours again.

15. They are camping in the valley.

16. Pete was here late in the evening.

6 **Homonyms:** here and hear

Can you hear the music?

Our guests are here.

Here are the records.

Did you _____ the news?

_____ is your car key.

Put the paper _____ .

I _____ the radio playing.

29

Practice 9-B: Long **e** (-eeze, -eese, -ease, -eeve, -eave)

1

/z/	/s/
breeze	
-eeze	
cheese	geese
-eese	**-eese**
please	lease
-ease	**-ease**

/v/

sleeve	leave
-eeve	**-eave**

2 Write the letters and say the word.

/z/		/s/	
br	_____ eeze	g	_____ eese
fr	_____ eeze	l	_____ ease
sn	_____ eeze	cr	_____ ease
squ	_____ eeze	gr	_____ ease
ch	_____ eese		

/v/

	_____ ease	sl	_____ eeve
t	_____ ease	l	_____ eave
pl	_____ ease	w	_____ eave

3 Read the words.

sneeze	lease
breeze	grease
squeeze	crease
freeze	geese
cheese	weave
tease	leave
ease	sleeve
please	

4 Write the word you hear.

1. _____   10. _____
2. _____   11. _____
3. _____   12. _____
4. _____   13. _____
5. _____   14. _____
6. _____   15. _____
7. _____
8. _____
9. _____

5 Read the sentences.   **New words:** easy, peace

1. Please rake these leaves.
2. It was not easy to keep the peace.
3. Dust makes me sneeze.
4. The rain will freeze to sleet.
5. She can weave a rug with ease.
6. Dee has a grease spot on her sleeve.
7. Do not tease him. Leave him in peace.
8. Pete squeezed my hand.
9. Cheese sandwiches are easy to make.
10. This apartment has a one-year lease.
11. We are hunting for geese.
12. That breeze feels good.
13. Leave me some pills to ease the pain.
14. Steve is always easy to please.
15. May she rest in peace.
16. She presses a crease into the pants.

6 Homonyms: <u>sea</u> and <u>see</u>

The boats are on the <u>sea</u>.

A blind man cannot <u>see</u>.

Let me <u>see</u> if I can help.

I need glasses to _____ it.

Do you _____ what I mean?

They are fishing in the _____ .

The ship sailed out to _____ .

Practice 10: Review of Long e

1 Look at the picture and say the word. Then write the word.

_____   _____ _____ _____   _____   _____

---

2 Circle all the words that are the same as the first one.

breed	bred	breed	bread	greed	bleed	breed	beer
dear	dear	dean	bear	dear	deer	read	dare
steal	steel	seal	steal	least	steal	steam	steal
these	the	these	those	there	tease	these	thee

3 Make at least *8* words with these beginnings and endings.

b   eer   _____ _____ _____

ch eal   _____ _____ _____

st eep   _____ _____ _____

m   eat   _____ _____ _____

4 Use these words to fill in the blanks:

> cream   turkey   sleep   bleach
> green   three   hear   east

1. You can clean these sheets with _____ .

2. Keep going _____ until you reach First Street.

3. Jean has beets, _____ beans, and peas in her garden.

4. Please speak more clearly. I cannot _____ you.

5. Here is _____ for the tea and coffee.

6. Steve sells meat — beef, veal, and _____ .

7. Pete was a speech teacher for _____ years.

8. Lee feels weak. He needs lots of _____ .

1

ride

side

-ide

five

drive

-ive

2 Write the letters and say the word.

h	_____ ide	d	_____ ive
r	_____ ide	f	_____ ive
s	_____ ide	h	_____ ive
t	_____ ide	l	_____ ive
w	_____ ide	dr	_____ ive
gu	_____ ide	str	_____ ive
sl	_____ ide		
br	_____ ide		
pr	_____ ide		

3 Read the words.

side	live
wide	hive
ride	drive
pride	strive
slide	five
hide	dive
bride	
tide	
guide	

4 Write the word you hear.

1. _____ 10. _____

2. _____ 11. _____

3. _____ 12. _____

4. _____ 13. _____

5. _____ 14. _____

6. _____ 15. _____

7. _____

8. _____

9. _____

5 Read the sentences. **New word:** beside **Review words:** driver, rider, license, bicycle

1. Jean dives into the deep water.

2. This rug is five feet wide.

3. You drive. I'll ride in the back.

4. Ed is hiding out on the east side.

5. Dad takes pride in his bee hives.

6. I have pictures and slides of my trip.

7. The guide stayed beside her.

8. The tide is coming in.

9. The TV guide is beside the lamp.

10. Did that bicycle rider win the race?

11. The hive was filled with live bees.

12. We slide down the side of the hill.

13. Grace just got her driver's license.

14. Dean's bride is standing beside him.

15. Five of us played hide and seek.

16. I strive hard to win.

6 Circle the letter for the vowel sound you hear.

1. i Ī		9. i Ī
2. i Ī		10. i Ī
3. i Ī		11. i Ī
4. i Ī		12. i Ī
5. i Ī		13. i Ī
6. i Ī		14. i Ī
7. i Ī		15. i Ī
8. i Ī		16. i Ī

1

line

nine

-ine

tribe

-ibe

2 Write the letters and say the word.

d	_____ ine	sh	_____ ine
f	_____ ine	sp	_____ ine
l	_____ ine	tw	_____ ine
m	_____ ine		
n	_____ ine		
p	_____ ine		
v	_____ ine		
w	_____ ine	br	_____ ibe
wh	_____ ine	tr	_____ ibe

3 Read the words.

pine	twine
wine	mine
nine	dine
fine	
shine	
vine	
whine	
spine	tribe
line	bribe

4 Write the word you hear.

1. _____   10. _____

2. _____   11. _____

3. _____   12. _____

4. _____   13. _____

5. _____   14. _____

6. _____

7. _____

8. _____

9. _____

5 Read the sentences.   **New word:** silver   **Review words:** Carla, month, written

1. The tree is covered with vines.

2. That silver dollar is mine, not yours.

3. It gets hot when the sun shines.

4. We drank fine wine as we dined.

5. Jean is working in a silver mine.

6. The little kids fuss and whine.

7. Carla planted a line of pine trees.

8. These Indians are from the same tribe.

9. The cop did not take the bribe.

10. Grapes on these vines are for wine.

11. Carla will shine our fine silver.

12. I fell on my back and hurt my spine.

13. It takes nine months to have a baby.

14. A name was written on the dotted line.

15. Carla paid a fine of nine dollars.

16. Cut off three feet of twine.

6 Circle the letter for the vowel sound you hear.

1. i ī   9. i ī

2. i ī   10. i ī

3. i ī   11. i ī

4. i ī   12. i ī

5. i ī   13. i ī

6. i ī   14. i ī

7. i ī   15. i ī

8. i ī   16. i ī

Practice 11-C: Long i (-ime, -ipe)

1

time
dime
-ime

ripe
pipe
-ipe

2 Write the letters and say the word.

d	_____ ime	p	_____ ipe
l	_____ ime	r	_____ ipe
t	_____ ime	w	_____ ipe
ch	_____ ime	gr	_____ ipe
sl	_____ ime	sw	_____ ipe
cr	_____ ime	str	_____ ipe
gr	_____ ime		

3 Read the words.

chime	ripe
time	pipe
crime	gripe
lime	wipe
grime	stripe
dime	swipe
slime	

4 Write the word you hear.

1. _____   10. _____
2. _____   11. _____
3. _____   12. _____
4. _____   13. _____
5. _____
6. _____
7. _____
8. _____
9. _____

5 Read the sentences.   **Review words:** written, angry, eye, test, bicycle

1. Stealing a bicycle is a crime.
2. It takes time for limes to get ripe.
3. Eve wipes the tears from her eyes.
4. Can you hear the church bells chime?
5. Jane is fixing a leaking water pipe.
   Her hands are covered with grime.
6. What time is it? Nine o'clock.
7. Steve paid a dime for one ripe apple.

8. Dean's shirt has red and green stripes.
9. I need another dime for a lime drink.
10. I ran out of time on the written test.
11. He swiped money from the cash box.
    The cops got him for that crime.
12. Dad lit up his pipe.
13. Wipe the slime off the fish tank.
14. You always gripe about your job.

6 Circle the letter for the vowel sound you hear.

1. i ī   9. i ī
2. i ī   10. i ī
3. i ī   11. i ī
4. i ī   12. i ī
5. i ī   13. i ī
6. i ī   14. i ī
7. i ī   15. i ī
8. i ī   16. i ī

Practice 12-A: Long i (-ice, -ike)

1

nice

price

-ice

like

Mike

-ike

2 Write the letters and say the word.

	ice	b			ike
d	___ ice	d		___	ike
m	___ ice	h		___	ike
n	___ ice	l		___	ike
r	___ ice	M		___	ike
sl	___ ice	sp		___	ike
pr	___ ice	str		___	ike
sp	___ ice				
tw	___ ice				

3 Read the words.

rice	like
spice	hike
nice	spike
ice	bike
price	strike
twice	dike
dice	Mike
slice	
mice	

4 Write the word you hear.

1. _____   10. _____

2. _____   11. _____

3. _____   12. _____

4. _____   13. _____

5. _____   14. _____

6. _____   15. _____

7. _____   16. _____

8. _____

9. _____

---

5 Read the sentences.   **Review words:** been, every, husband

1. Have a slice of spice cake.

2. Mike strikes out every time at bat.

3. Shake the dice.

4. The price of gas has been going up.

5. This is a nice day to take a hike.

6. Did the car strike the bike rider?

7. My husband likes to ice skate.

8. Mike eats rice twice a day.

9. A spike is a large nail.

10. Mike's bike looks just like mine.

11. This ice cream sells for half price.

12. This spice rack will make a nice gift.

13. Dice the meat and add it to the rice.

14. The mice have been eating the cheese.

15. The dike held back the water.

16. Every worker went on strike.

6 Circle the letter for the vowel sound you hear.

1. i T̄   9. i T̄

2. i T̄   10. i T̄

3. i T̄   11. i T̄

4. i T̄   12. i T̄

5. i T̄   13. i T̄

6. i T̄   14. i T̄

7. i T̄   15. i T̄

8. i T̄   16. i T̄

Practice 12-B: Long i (-ile, -ite)

1

mile

while

-ile

bite

white

-ite

2 Write the letters and say the word.

f _____ ile   b _____ ite

m _____ ile   k _____ ite

p _____ ile   qu _____ ite

t _____ ile   s _____ ite

wh _____ ile   wh _____ ite

sm _____ ile   wr _____ ite

3 Read the words.

pile   kite

while   site

mile   write

smile   bite

tile   quite

file   white

4 Write the word you hear.

1. _____   10. _____

2. _____   11. _____

3. _____   12. _____

4. _____

5. _____

6. _____

7. _____

8. _____

9. _____

5 Read the sentences.   **Review words:** race, sign, sometimes, written, White

1. The sign says the city is a mile away.

2. Mike smiles when he greets people.

3. Look at that pile of papers!

   File them while I sign these letters.

4. I did quite well in the five-mile race.

5. I'll get a bite to eat while you shop.

6. Sign the check. Write your name here.

7. They will build a school on that site.

8. The letter was written on white paper.

9. Mrs. White files her nails.

10. Sometimes I cannot read your writing.

11. Did that pup bite him?

12. Rake this pile of leaves.

13. He has not written in quite a while.

14. Jason's kite is up in the air.

15. Let's put white tiles in the kitchen.

6 Circle the letter for the vowel sound you hear.

1. i ī   9. i ī

2. i ī   10. i ī

3. i ī   11. i ī

4. i ī   12. i ī

5. i ī   13. i ī

6. i ī   14. i ī

7. i ī   15. i ī

8. i ī   16. i ī

Practice 12-C: Long i (-ife, -ire, -ives, -ise, -ize)

1

life   lives
wife   wives
-ife   **-ives**

tire   wise
-ire   **-ise**

        size
        -ize

2 Write the letters and say the word.

l _____ ife	l _____ ives
w _____ ife	w _____ ives
kn _____ ife	kn _____ ives
f _____ ire	r _____ ise
h _____ ire	w _____ ise
t _____ ire	
w _____ ire	s _____ ize
	pr _____ ize

3 Read the words.

wife	wives
knife	lives
life	knives
wire	wise
hire	rise
fire	
tire	prize
	size

4 Write the word you hear.

1. _____ 10. _____
2. _____ 11. _____
3. _____ 12. _____
4. _____ 13. _____
5. _____ 14. _____
6. _____
7. _____
8. _____
9. _____

5 Read the sentences.   **Review words:** tired, retired, been, husband, eye

1. That dress is a size eighteen.
2. Put the knives on the table.
3. He has been retired for five years.
4. Bad wires can start a fire!
5. Mike is tired of city life.
6. It's wise to check the air in my tires.
7. Hire a person to fix these wires.
8. Some husbands leave their wives.

9. Cut the turkey with a sharp knife.
10. A lot of reading can tire your eyes.
11. His wife lived a happy life.
12. Dee hired six people and fired two.
13. The sun rises in the east.
14. Seat belts save many lives.
15. He was tired after running the race.
     But he did win first prize!

6 Circle the letter for the vowel sound you hear.

1. i Ī	9. i Ī
2. i Ī	10. i Ī
3. i Ī	11. i Ī
4. i Ī	12. i Ī
5. i Ī	13. i Ī
6. i Ī	14. i Ī
7. i Ī	15. i Ī
8. i Ī	16. i Ī

37

Practice 13-A: Long i (-y)

1

by

cry

dry

-y

2 Write the letters and say the word.

b _____ y   pr _____ y

m _____ y   tr _____ y

sh _____ y   sk _____ y

wh _____ y   sp _____ y

fl _____ y

sl _____ y

cr _____ y

dr _____ y

fr _____ y

3 Read the words.

cry	by
sky	pry
why	shy
try	sly
my	
fry	
spy	
fly	
dry	

4 Write the word you hear.

1. _____   10. _____

2. _____   11. _____

3. _____   12. _____

4. _____   13. _____

5. _____

6. _____

7. _____

8. _____

9. _____

5 Read the sentences.   **Review words:** o'clock, written

1. Why is she so shy?

2. You must dry-clean this dress.

3. He is trying to spy on us.

4. Tell me why you are crying.

5. The sky is clearing.

6. Try to pry the lid off this crate.

7. A fly is on the table.

8. Dave will fry the fish in hot fat.

9. That letter was written by my wife.

10. We can see birds flying in the sky.

11. The frying pan is by the sink.

12. I dry the dishes with this rag.

13. He gave me a sly look.

14. I heard my son cry out.

15. I'll try to be back by five o'clock.

16. She hit a pop-up fly to first base.

6 Circle the letter for the vowel sound you hear.

1. a ī   9. a ī

2. a ī   10. a ī

3. a ī   11. a ī

4. a ī   12. a ī

5. a ī   13. a ī

6. a ī   14. a ī

7. a ī   15. a ī

8. a ī   16. a ī

Practice 13-B: Long i (-ie, -ye, -y – e)

1

die
tie
-ie

eye
-ye

type
-y -e

2 Write the letters and say the word.

d _____ ie   t _____ ype

l _____ ie

p _____ ie   st _____ yle

t _____ ie

rh _____ yme

e _____ ye

d _____ ye

l _____ ye

r _____ ye

3 Read the words.

pie   style

die

tie   rhyme

lie

             type

lye

rye

eye

dye

4 Write the word you hear.

1. _____   10. _____

2. _____   11. _____

3. _____

4. _____

5. _____

6. _____

7. _____

8. _____

9. _____

5 Read the sentences.   **New words:** buy, guy

1. Grace is very sick. She may die.

2. Mike put on a green and white tie.

3. Lee never tells any lies.

4. Buy some rye bread at the market.

5. My husband is a very nice guy.

6. Tie up the box with string.

7. What type of pie do you like best?

8. The dresses I buy are always in style.

9. Lye can burn your eyes and skin.

10. The game ended in a tie.

11. This apple pie was a good buy.

12. The eye doctor says I need glasses.

13. That guy can type very fast.

14. Lie on the bed and rest for a while.

15. Jane wants to dye her hair red.

16. Do these words rhyme?

6 Homonyms: dye and die

Dye the shirt dark blue.

Did he die in the accident?

Mix up the red _____ .

The sick man may _____ .

I will _____ the dress green.

Did they _____ in the fire?

Practice 13-C: Endings -s, -ed, -ing

-s To put the -s ending on words with Consonant + y, change the y to i. Then add -es.

cry
cri + es ⟶ cries

1 Put the -s ending on these words. Read the words.

fly _____

cry _____

fry _____

try _____

sky _____

spy _____

2 Put the -s ending on these action words and fill in the blank. Read the sentences.

1. dry   Dad _____ the dishes.

2. fly   Eve _____ the plane.

3. try   The robber _____ to hide.

4. fry   She _____ two eggs.

5. cry   Ann _____ at every wedding.

6. pry   Steve _____ open the box.

3 Take off the -s ending and write the root word.

tries _____

flies _____

spies _____

dries _____

skies _____

fries _____

-ed To put the -ed ending on words with Consonant + y, change the y to i. Then add -ed.

dry
dri + ed ⟶ dried

4 Put the -ed ending on these words. Read the words.

try _____

spy _____

cry _____

dry _____

fry _____

5 Put the -ed ending on these action words and fill in the blank. Read the sentences.

1. fry   I _____ some potatoes.

2. cry   The baby _____ out.

3. dry   Jane _____ her eyes.

4. spy   Lee _____ on them.

5. try   The team _____ to win.

6 Take off the -ed ending and write the root word.

dried _____

tried _____

spied _____

fried _____

cried _____

-ing   Just add the *-ing* ending to all words ending with *y*. Do not change the root word.

fry + ing ⟶ frying

---

7 | Put the *-ing* ending on these words. Read the words.

dry _____

try _____

fly _____

cry _____

spy _____

fry _____

pry _____

8 | Put the *-ing* ending on these action words and fill in the blank. Read the sentences.

1. pry   Jim is _____ the lid off.

2. cry   Do you hear her _____ .

3. dry   The sun is _____ out the plants.

4. try   Dee is _____ to work.

5. fly   Birds are _____ over us.

6. spy   Is he _____ on me?

7. fry   The meat is _____ in hot fat.

9 | Take off the *-ing* ending. Write the root word.

flying _____

prying _____

spying _____

frying _____

trying _____

drying _____

crying _____

10

-ed   To put the *-ed* ending on words that end with *e*, just add a *d*.

tie + d ⟶ tied

Put the *-ed* ending on these words. Read the sentences.

1. die   He _____ last year.

2. lie   Kay _____ about her age.

3. tie   Mike _____ the string.

11

-ing   To put the *-ing* ending on words that end with *ie*, change the *ie* to *y* and then add *-ing*.

die
dy + ing ⟶ dying

Put the *-ing* ending on these words. Read the words.

1. die   The sick man is _____ .

2. lie   Have you been _____ to me?

3. tie   She is _____ back her hair.

12

Take off the *-ed* or *-ing* ending. Write the root word.

tied _____

died _____

lied _____

dying _____

lying _____

tying _____

41

Practice 14-A: Long i (-igh, -ight)

1

high

-igh

night

sight

-ight

2 Write the letters and say the word.

h ___ igh	m ___ ight
s ___ igh	n ___ ight
th ___ igh	r ___ ight
	s ___ ight
	t ___ ight
	fl ___ ight
f ___ ight	sl ___ ight
he ___ ight	br ___ ight
l ___ ight	fr ___ ight

3 Read the words.

sigh	fight
high	right
thigh	tight
	might
	fright
	slight
light	bright
sight	height
night	flight

4 Write the word you hear.

1. _____   10. _____
2. _____   11. _____
3. _____   12. _____
4. _____   13. _____
5. _____   14. _____
6. _____   15. _____
7. _____
8. _____
9. _____

5 Read the sentences.   **New words:** tonight   **Review words:** I'm, arrive, been, TV

1. These light green slacks are not tight.
   They fit right. But the price is high.

2. Tonight I'm watching the fights on TV.

3. Check on this plane flight right away.

4. At night the stars shine. What a sight!

5. He is very bright. He gets high marks.

6. Her flight arrives at nine tonight.

7. Do you want a wing or a thigh to eat?

8. That mask gave me a fright!

9. Jean's height is five feet one inch.

10. That box is light. You can lift it.

11. The bright lights are still in sight.

12. Lee had a slight cut on his right arm.

    "I got in a fight tonight," said Lee.

    "Fighting is not right," sighed Mom.

    "You might have been hurt badly!"

6 Homonyms: right and write

Write me a note right now!

She writes with her right hand.

Every answer on the test is right.

This soup tastes just right.

Stealing is not _____ .

We _____ letters every day.

Jean hurt her _____ leg.

Do your math _____ this time.

42

Practice 14-B: Long i (-ind, -ild)

1

find
kind
-ind

child
mild
-ild

2 Write the letters and say the word.

b _____ ind   m _____ ild

f _____ ind   w _____ ild

h _____ ind   ch _____ ild

k _____ ind

m _____ ind

w _____ ind

bl _____ ind

gr _____ ind

3 Read the words.

mind	child
kind	mild
blind	wild
wind	
grind	
bind	
find	
hind	

4 Write the word you hear.

1. _____   10. _____

2. _____   11. _____

3. _____

4. _____

5. _____

6. _____

7. _____

8. _____

9. _____

5 Read the sentences.   **New word:** pint   **Review words:** OK, behind, quart, gallon

1. Get a pint of ice cream. Any kind is OK.

2. We had a mild summer this year.

3. The teacher is very kind to my child.

   She always finds time to help him.

4. I have a lot of things on my mind.

5. My child drinks a pint of milk a day.

   I buy milk in pints, quarts, or gallons.

6. He never seems to mind if I get behind.

7. They are hunting wild geese.

8. The blind man cannot find our street.

9. That is a very mild cheese.

10. The pup has a cut on its hind leg.

11. Wind your watch. It's running behind.

12. That child never minds his father.

13. Please grind up that beef for me.

14. The pages came out of the binding.

6 Homonyms: buy and by

He can buy it by getting a loan.

Get home by eight o'clock.

Put your books by the chair.

Mike sat _____ his sister.

The days go _____ so fast

I want to _____ a new car.

Dean will be here _____ six.

43

Practice 15: Review of Long i

1 Look at the picture and say the word. Then write the word.

_____ _____ _____ _____ _____ _____

2 Circle all the words that are the same as the first one.

ripe	ride	ripe	pier	rip	ripe	pipe	ripe
hike	bike	hide	hike	hiker	dike	hike	like
mind	mind	mine	mint	mind	wind	mild	dime
sight	sigh	might	sight	sign	slight	right	sight

3 Make at least *10* words with these beginnings and endings:

pr ide   _____ _____ _____

m ight   _____ _____ _____

sl y   _____ _____ _____

t ice   _____ _____ _____

4 Use these words to fill in the blanks:

mine   size   flight   find

life   dry   type   mile

1. He hides his money so we cannot _____ it.

2. What was your time in the five- _____ race?

3. This white dress is just the right _____ .

4. Stop crying. _____ your eyes.

5. That bright red bike is _____ .

6. _____ these letters. Then I'll sign them.

7. I risked my _____ fighting the fire.

8. I'll arrive on the nine o'clock _____ .

Practice 16-A: Long o (-o, -oe)

1

go

so

-o

toe

Joe

-oe

2 Write the letters and say the word.

g _____ o   d _____ oe

n _____ o   f _____ oe

s _____ o   h _____ oe

pr _____ o   t _____ oe

                     J _____ oe

3 Read the words.

no	Joe
pro	hoe
go	doe
so	foe
	toe

4 Write the word you hear.

1. _____

2. _____

3. _____

4. _____

5. _____

6. _____

7. _____

8. _____

9. _____

5 Read the sentences.   **New words:** goes, also, shoe   **Review word:** we'll

1. Can I go? Say yes or no!

2. Joe teaches math. I teach it also.

3. He goes to the shed to get the hoe.

4. I hurt my toe in the race a week ago.

5. The doe takes care of her baby deer.

6. This car goes fast. It is also cheap.

7. He quit the pro hockey team a year ago.

8. This shoe fits well from heel to toe.

9. Joe takes pictures of the doe.

10. If she goes, we'll go also.

11. He worked in a shoe store a year ago.

12. I have no money, so I need a job.

13. We take lessons from a real pro.

14. These shoes hurt my toes.

15. Joe died a month ago. We miss him so!

16. Are you a friend or a foe?

6 Circle the letter for the vowel sound you hear.

1. o   ō   9. o   ō

2. o   ō   10. o   ō

3. o   ō   11. o   ō

4. o   ō   12. o   ō

5. o   ō   13. o   ō

6. o   ō   14. o   ō

7. o   ō   15. o   ō

8. o   ō   16. o   ō

1

old
told
gold
-old

colt
-olt

roll
-oll

2 Write the letters and say the word.

	old	sc	____	old
b	____ old			
c	____ old	b	____ olt
f	____ old	c	____ olt
g	____ old	j	____ olt
h	____ old	v	____ olt
m	____ old			
s	____ old	r	____ oll
t	____ old	t	____ oll

3 Read the words.

gold	fold
mold	
cold	jolt
sold	bolt
old	volt
scold	colt
told	
bold	toll
hold	roll

4 Write the word you hear.

1. _____   10. _____
2. _____   11. _____
3. _____   12. _____
4. _____   13. _____
5. _____   14. _____
6. _____   15. _____
7. _____   16. _____
8. _____
9. _____

5 Read the sentences. **Review words:** open, Tony, door, battery

1. These dinner rolls are getting cold.
2. I scolded him for tracking in mud.
3. We must pay a toll every ten miles.
4. This old bread is covered with mold.
5. That bolt holds the door shut.
6. The leaves are turning red and gold.
7. The slaves made a bold escape.
8. What he told us gave us quite a jolt.
9. The letter was folded. I opened it.
10. Tony told the pup to roll over.
11. Tony can tame the wild colt.
12. Jake sold me an old gold ring.
13. That old woman has a bad cold.
14. Tony needs a 12-volt battery.
15. Mom put the ice cream into the mold.
16. She told me to fold the shirts.

6 Circle the letter for the vowel sound you hear.

1. o ō   9. o ō
2. o ō   10. o ō
3. o ō   11. o ō
4. o ō   12. o ō
5. o ō   13. o ō
6. o ō   14. o ō
7. o ō   15. o ō
8. o ō   16. o ō

Practice 17-A: Long o (-ole, -oke)

1

hole
stole
-ole

woke
smoke
-oke

2 Write the letters and say the word.

h	_____ ole	j	_____ oke
m	_____ ole	p	_____ oke
p	_____ ole	w	_____ oke
r	_____ ole	ch	_____ oke
s	_____ ole	br	_____ oke
st	_____ ole	sm	_____ oke
wh	_____ ole	sp	_____ oke
		str	_____ oke

3 Read the words.

hole	choke
role	woke
stole	broke
pole	joke
whole	spoke
mole	poke
sole	stroke
	smoke

4 Write the word you hear.

1. _____   10. _____
2. _____   11. _____
3. _____   12. _____
4. _____   13. _____
5. _____   14. _____
6. _____   15. _____
7. _____
8. _____
9. _____

5 Read the sentences.   **Review words:** both, don't, stolen

1. We don't like his jokes.
2. He choked on the smoke from the fire.
3. Tony's fishing pole has been stolen!
4. Grandmother had a bad stroke.

   She was in bed for a whole month.
5. The mole dug a deep hole in the dirt.
6. Mike fell and broke both his arms.
7. What role will he act in the play?

8. Dad tells his son, "Don't smoke!"
9. We both woke up at six o'clock.
10. Tony strokes the cat's head.
11. I was broke after I paid the rent.
12. The kids stole a whole apple pie!
13. Joe woke up when his wife poked him.
14. Dee spoke to Joe last week.
15. Put new soles on these shoes.

6 **Homonyms:** <u>hole</u> and <u>whole</u>

A doughnut has a <u>hole</u> in the middle.

The golf ball went into the <u>hole</u>.

The <u>whole</u> class went on the trip.

Two halves make one <u>whole</u>.

He dug a _____ two feet deep.

I ate a _____ cake.

We worked on it a _____ week.

This sock has a _____ in it.

Practice 17-B: Long o (-one, -ope, -ode)

1

stone

phone

-one

hope

-ope

rode

-ode

2 Write the letters and say the word.

b ____ one	d ____ ope
c ____ one	h ____ ope
l ____ one	m ____ ope
t ____ one	p ____ ope
z ____ one	r ____ ope
sh ____ one	sl ____ ope
thr ____ one	
st ____ one	c ____ ode
ph ____ one	r ____ ode

3 Read the words.

tone	pope
shone	hope
zone	slope
phone	rope
bone	dope
stone	mope
cone	
throne	rode
lone	code

4 Write the word you hear.

1. _____   10. _____

2. _____   11. _____

3. _____   12. _____

4. _____   13. _____

5. _____   14. _____

6. _____   15. _____

7. _____   16. _____

8. _____   17. _____

9. _____

5 Read the sentences.   **Review words:** don't, Stone, alone, broken, angry

1. Don't you want an ice cream cone?

2. A light shone in the dark.

3. She spoke in an angry tone.

4. He was selling dope and pills.

5. I have broken a bone! Phone Dr. Stone.

6. Don't give up hope. You are not alone.

7. The king sat on his throne.

8. One lone car is in the no-parking zone.

9. This letter is written in code.

10. The big stones rolled down the slope.

11. Lee flunked math. But he is no dope.

12. Tie it up with this rope.

13. The pope spoke to the people.

14. Tony rode past a school zone.

15. We hope to have a new phone put in.

16. He sits alone and mopes.

6 Circle the letter for the vowel sound you hear.

1. o   ō   9. o   ō

2. o   ō   10. o   ō

3. o   ō   11. o   ō

4. o   ō   12. o   ō

5. o   ō   13. o   ō

6. o   ō   14. o   ō

7. o   ō   15. o   ō

8. o   ō   16. o   ō

Practice 17-C: Long o (-obe, -ove, -ote, -ome)

1

robe
-obe
stove
-ove
note
-ote
home
-ome

2 Write the letters and say the word.

r _____ obe   n _____ ote

gl _____ obe   qu _____ ote

v _____ ote

wr _____ ote

d _____ ove

w _____ ove

dr _____ ove   d _____ ome

gr _____ ove   h _____ ome

st _____ ove   R _____ ome

3 Read the words.

globe   vote

robe   wrote

note

quote

stove

dove

grove   Rome

wove   dome

drove   home

4 Write the word you hear.

1. _____   10. _____

2. _____   11. _____

3. _____   12. _____

4. _____   13. _____

5. _____   14. _____

6. _____

7. _____

8. _____

9. _____

5 Read the sentences.   **Review words:** that's, hundred

1. I wrote a note to my friend.

2. The bus driver drove a hundred miles.

3. Heat it up on the stove.

4. Tony dove into the water.

5. That building has a dome on top of it.

6. Play the first five notes.

7. Can you find Rome on this globe?

8. She got out of bed and put on a robe.

9. We drove home after the hockey game.

10. We have a gas stove at home.

11. That's the person I'll vote for.

12. She wove a rug out of old yarn.

13. Joe wrote a note home every week.

14. That's good! May I quote you?

15. Did you vote this year?

16. My home is near a grove of trees.

6 Circle the letter for the vowel sound you hear.

1. u ō   9. u ō

2. u ō   10. u ō

3. u ō   11. u ō

4. u ō   12. u ō

5. u ō   13. u ō

6. u ō   14. u ō

7. u ō   15. u ō

8. u ō   16. u ō

Practice 17-D: Long o (-ose, -oze)

1

/z/

nose

rose

-ose

froze

-oze

/s/

close

-ose

2 Write the letters and say the word.

/z/		/z/	
h _____ ose		d _____ oze	
n _____ ose		fr _____ oze	
p _____ ose			
r _____ ose			
ch _____ ose		**/s/**	
th _____ ose		d _____ ose	
cl _____ ose		cl _____ ose	
R _____ ose			

3 Read the words.

/z/	/z/
rose	froze
those	doze
hose	
close	
pose	
Rose	**/s/**
chose	close
nose	dose

4 Write the word you hear.

1. _____ 10. _____

2. _____ 11. _____

3. _____ 12. _____

4. _____

5. _____

6. _____

7. _____

8. _____

9. _____

5 Read the sentences.   **Review word:** door

1. He chose those red roses.

2. I was standing close to the door.

3. The water pipes froze last night.

4. My nose is stuffed up. I have a cold.

5. She chose ten women for the team.

6. Those doors will not close.

7. Rose will pose for the picture.

8. Water the roses with this garden hose.

9. Those stores close at five o'clock.

10. He takes a large dose of the drug.

11. People rose when the judge came in.

12. That man is posing as a doctor.

13. His eyes closed. He started to doze.

14. I need to buy a new pair of hose.

15. We skated on the lake after it froze.

16. Rose and Tony sat close together.

6 Circle the letter for the vowel sound you hear.

1. u   ō   9. u   ō

2. u   ō   10. u   ō

3. u   ō   11. u   ō

4. u   ō   12. u   ō

5. u   ō   13. u   ō

6. u   ō   14. u   ō

7. u   ō   15. u   ō

8. u   ō   16. u   ō

Practice 18-A: Long o (-oat, -oal, -oak, -oad)

1

boat

-oat

coal

-oal

soak

-oak

road

-oad

2 Write the letters and say the word.

		oat			oak
b	___	oat	s	___	oak
c	___	oat	cl	___	oak
g	___	oat	cr	___	oak
fl	___	oat			
thr	___	oat			
			l	___	oad
c	___	oal	r	___	oad
g	___	oal	t	___	oad

3 Read the words.

goat	croak
oat	soak
float	oak
boat	cloak
throat	
coat	
	toad
goal	road
coal	load

4 Write the word you hear.

1. _____ 10. _____

2. _____ 11. _____

3. _____ 12. _____

4. _____ 13. _____

5. _____ 14. _____

6. _____ 15. _____

7. _____

8. _____

9. _____

5 Read the sentences.　　**New word:** soap　　**Review words:** over, clothes

1. We burn coal to heat our home.

2. Our boat didn't float. We got soaked!

3. The coat has a stain. Rub soap on it.

4. A truck carried the load up the road.

5. The toad is croaking.

6. That farmer raises sheep and goats.

7. Joe was the first to reach the goal.

8. Soak the clothes in soap and water.

9. Tony fed oats to the horses.

10. A bone got stuck in her throat.

11. The table is made of oak.

12. She put a cloak on over her clothes.

13. I chased the goat down the road.

14. The hunter is loading his gun.

15. The bar of soap floats in the water.

16. Rose put a coat of paint on the boat.

6 **Homonyms:** road and rode

I rode the bus for an hour.

We rode on a very bumpy road.

Tony _____ on the train.

The car went off the _____ .

I _____ my bike to work.

This _____ is not very wide.

Practice 18-B: Long o (-oan, -oast, -oam, -oach, -oaf, -oaves)

1

Joan coach

-oan -oach

toast loaf

-oast -oaf

foam loaves

-oam -oaves

2 Write the letters and say the word.

l	_____ oan	f	_____ oam
m	_____ oan	r	_____ oam
gr	_____ oan		
J	_____ oan	c	_____ oach
		r	_____ oach
b	_____ oast	p	_____ oach
c	_____ oast		
r	_____ oast	l	_____ oaf
t	_____ oast	l	_____ oaves

3 Read the words.

moan	roam
Joan	foam
loan	
groan	poach
	roach
roast	coach
boast	
toast	loaf
coast	loaves

4 Write the word you hear.

1._____	10._____
2._____	11._____
3._____	12._____
4._____	13._____
5._____	14._____
6._____	15._____
7._____	
8._____	
9._____	

5 Read the sentences.   **Review words:** over, sofa, rubber

1. The bank will loan her the money.
2. Joan boasts about her roast beef.
3. The sofa is filled with foam rubber.
4. Give me a poached egg on toast.
5. The sick man moans and groans.
6. Joan is our new track coach.
7. The boat sailed up the coast.
8. This spray will kill the roaches.

9. Tony toasted rolls over the fire.
10. Our dog likes to roam in the park.
11. He coasted down the hill on his sled.
12. I want a loaf of whole wheat bread.
    And give me two loaves of rye bread.
13. I roasted the meat over the hot coals.
14. When I asked for a loan, he groaned.
15. He coaches the hockey team.

6 **Homonyms:** <u>clothes</u> and <u>close</u>

<u>Close</u> the window

Bring this meeting to a <u>close</u>.

I'll wash these <u>clothes</u>.

Those stores _____ at six.

Please _____ the door.

He put on old _____ .

Are those _____ clean?

Practice 19-A: Long o (-ow)

1

show

blow

know

-ow

below

yellow

window

2 Write the letters and say the word.

		owe	bl	_____ ow
b	_____ ow		fl	_____ ow
l	_____ ow		gl	_____ ow
m	_____ ow		sl	_____ ow
r	_____ ow		cr	_____ ow
s	_____ ow		gr	_____ ow
t	_____ ow		sn	_____ ow
kn	_____ ow		thr	_____ ow
sh	_____ ow			

3 Read the words.

snow	grow
row	show
flow	low
crow	throw
know	slow
bow	tow
glow	blow
owe	mow
sow	

4 Write the word you hear.

1. _____   10. _____
2. _____   11. _____
3. _____   12. _____
4. _____   13. _____
5. _____   14. _____
6. _____   15. _____
7. _____   16. _____
8. _____   17. _____
9. _____

5 Read the sentences.   **Review words:** onto, yellow, window, below, follow, slowly, speed

1. Slow down! Keep your speed low.
2. Follow me. I'll show you the way.
3. The bright light glows in the dark.
4. Joan is throwing stones at the crows.
5. The farmer sows the seeds in rows.
6. My car broke down. I need a tow truck.
7. The river flows into the valley below.
8. Those plants grow very slowly.
9. Joe knows he owes me five dollars.
10. The two of us will row the boat.
11. Do you know when that TV show is on?
12. This grass grows fast. I'll mow it.
13. The plane is flying low.
14. The wind blows snow onto the road.
15. Look out the window. It's snowing!
16. Her dress has a yellow bow in back.

6 **Homonyms:** <u>tow</u> and <u>toe</u>

Those shoes have pointed <u>toes</u>.

Tie a rope to the boat and <u>tow</u> it.

He stepped on my _____ .

The truck can _____ your car.

_____ the boat back home.

Joan's _____ is broken.

Practice 19-B: Long o (-own, -owl, -owth)

1

own
blown
known
-own
bowl
-owl
growth
-owth

2 Write the letters and say the word.

	own	b	_____ owl
kn	_____ own		
sh	_____ own		
fl	_____ own		
bl	_____ own		
gr	_____ own		
thr	_____ own	gr	_____ owth

3 Read the words.

blown	bowl
shown	
grown	
own	
thrown	
flown	
known	growth

4 Write the word you hear.

1. _____
2. _____
3. _____
4. _____
5. _____
6. _____
7. _____
8. _____
9. _____

5 Read the sentences.   **Review word:** you're

1. Whip the mix in a large bowl.
2. The plane has flown to Rome.
3. Mom bakes her own bread.
4. You're known for your fine speeches.
5. Those old clothes were thrown out.
6. My children have grown up so fast!
7. The papers were blown off my desk.
8. I own that yellow boat.
9. We want to stop the growth of crime.
10. Joan has shown us the big city.
11. You're on the best bowling team.
12. My plans were not known to them.
13. Have the birds flown away?
14. We stopped when the whistle was blown.
15. Joe was thrown from his horse.
16. I cut down a thick growth of weeds.

6 **Homonyms:** <u>grown</u> and <u>groan</u>

The trees had <u>grown</u> taller.

Stop moaning and <u>groaning</u>!

The city has _____ bigger.

Joe has _____ an inch.

A sharp pain made him _____ .

The sick man let out a _____ .

Practice 20-A: Long o (-or, -ore)

1

or
for
-or

more
store
-ore

2 Write the letters and say the word.

	or	s _____ ore	
f _____ or		t _____ ore	
n _____ or		w _____ ore	
		sh _____ ore	
	ore	ch _____ ore	
b _____ ore		sc _____ ore	
c _____ ore		sn _____ ore	
m _____ ore		st _____ ore	
p _____ ore		sw _____ ore	

3 Read the words.

for	core
or	shore
nor	ore
	swore
more	store
sore	bore
chore	score
snore	pore
wore	tore

4 Write the word you hear.

1. _____ 10. _____
2. _____ 11. _____
3. _____ 12. _____
4. _____ 13. _____
5. _____ 14. _____
6. _____ 15. _____
7. _____ 16. _____
8. _____ 17. _____
9. _____

5 Read the sentences.   **Review words:** before, than, most, four, player

1. I'll get more milk at the store.
2. Peel and core these four apples.
3. Tony snored for most of the night.
4. Do those chores before you leave.
5. Did I pass or fail? What was my score?
6. He swore he had not lied or cheated.
7. Joe tore his shirt at work.
8. Rose is bored in most of her classes.

9. She swam more than a mile to shore.
10. Joan tore open the four letters.
11. I pay more for gas than I did before.
12. The shoes I wore made my feet sore.
13. Can we get much ore from that mine?
14. Soap cleans the pores of the skin.
15. We store canned goods on this shelf.
16. I have never married, nor do I want to.

6 **Homonyms:** <u>for</u> and <u>four</u>

Here are <u>four</u> letters <u>for</u> you.

He sells apples <u>for</u> a quarter.

We worked there <u>for</u> a year.

He was jailed <u>for</u> his crimes.

These gifts are _____ you.

Did you vote _____ her?

The shirt costs _____ dollars.

Ask Ed _____ some money.

55

Practice 20-B: Long o (-ort, -orm, -ork, -ord)

1

short
-ort
storm
-orm
fork
-ork
cord
-ord

2 Write the letters and say the word.

f _____ ort   c _____ ork

p _____ ort   f _____ ork

s _____ ort   p _____ ork

sh _____ ort   st _____ ork

sn _____ ort   Y _____ ork

sp _____ ort

c _____ ord

f _____ orm   l _____ ord

st _____ orm   L _____ ord

3 Read the words.

short	pork
port	stork
sort	York
fort	cork
sport	fork
snort	
	lord
storm	cord
form	Lord

4 Write the word you hear.

1. _____   10. _____

2. _____   11. _____

3. _____   12. _____

4. _____   13. _____

5. _____   14. _____

6. _____   15. _____

7. _____   16. _____

8. _____

9. _____

5 Read the sentences.   **Review word:** order

1. Joe tripped over the phone cord.

2. I ordered pork chops for dinner.

3. The sports fans formed their own club.

4. Sort these letters. Put them in order.

5. Set the knives and forks on the table.

6. We visited an old fort in New York.

7. A lord was a man who owned much land.

8. The stork is a very large bird.

9. We fill out the short form for taxes.

10. The boats sailed into the port.

11. The storm lasted just a short while.

12. Father Dean prayed to the Lord.

13. Order storm windows from this store.

14. The horse is snorting.

15. What sort of sports do you like?

16. Put the cork back in the jug.

6 Homonyms: <u>no</u> and <u>know</u>

<u>No</u>, I don't <u>know</u> how to drive.

I didn't <u>know</u> he was sick.

<u>No</u> one <u>knows</u> your dad.

Do you _____ these words?

Joan has _____ job.

I _____ where she is.

Will you vote yes or _____ ?

Practice 20-C: Long o (-orn, -orth, -orch, -orge)

1

corn
born
-orn
north
-orth
porch
-orch
forge
-orge

2 Write the letters and say the word.

b ____ orn   n ____ orth

c ____ orn   f ____ orth

h ____ orn

t ____ orn   p ____ orch

w ____ orn   t ____ orch

th ____ orn   sc ____ orch

sc ____ orn

sw ____ orn   f ____ orge

                    g ____ orge

3 Read the words.

worn	forth
horn	north
thorn	
corn	torch
sworn	scorch
born	porch
torn	
scorn	gorge
	forge

4 Write the word you hear.

1. _____   10. _____

2. _____   11. _____

3. _____   12. _____

4. _____   13. _____

5. _____   14. _____

6. _____   15. _____

7. _____

8. _____

9. _____

5 Read the sentences.   **New word:** George   **Review words:** corner, want, someone, fourth

1. I was born on May fourth in New York.

2. These clothes are worn out or torn.

3. Roses have thorns on their stems.

4. George sat on the back porch.

   He rocked his chair back and forth.

5. That goat has horns on its head.

6. Did someone forge her name on a check?

7. Press the shirt, but don't scorch it.

8. Dee made her son sit in the corner.

9. George wants to play his new horn.

10. The runner carried a lighted torch.

11. The woman was sworn into office.

12. George picked ten ears of corn.

13. A gorge is a deep valley.

14. They looked at us with scorn.

15. Turn north at the fourth corner.

6 Homonyms: <u>forth</u> and <u>fourth</u>

The boy ran back and <u>forth</u>.

He came <u>forth</u> to confess.

This is the <u>fourth</u> job I've had.

I was the _____ one in line.

Math is my _____ class.

The players ran back and _____ .

The buds burst _____ .

Practice 20-D: Long o (-oar, -oard, -oarse, -orse, -orce)

1

roar

-oar

board

-oard

hoarse

-oarse

horse

-orse

force

-orce

2 Write the letters and say the word.

	oar	h _____ orse
b _____ oar		
r _____ oar	f _____ orce
s _____ oar		
b _____ oard		
c _____ oarse		
h _____ oarse		

3 Read the words.

soar   horse

roar

oar   force

boar

board

hoarse

coarse

4 Write the word you hear.

1. _____
2. _____
3. _____
4. _____
5. _____
6. _____
7. _____
8. _____
9. _____

5 Read the sentences.   **Review words:** Porter, fourth, door, floor, police, story, stories

1. She rows the boat with two oars.
2. Do not force that horse to go faster.
3. She wrote the story on the board.
4. Joe Porter owns that horse.
5. A boar is a wild pig.
6. Her throat was sore. She was hoarse.
7. We heard the car roar down the street.
8. Nail down those floor boards.

9. The birds soar high in the sky.
10. George Porter quit the police force.
11. That building is ten stories high.
    Mrs. Porter lives on the fourth floor.
12. Can we force open the apartment door?
13. We roared at the funny story he told.
14. This sand is coarse, not fine.
15. The police ride horses in our city.

6 Homonyms: <u>hoarse</u> and <u>horse</u>

Tony has a <u>hoarse</u> voice.

The <u>horse</u> pulled the wagon.

Did you ride that _____ ?

This sore throat makes me _____ .

His _____ ran in the race.

Listen to me. I'm _____ .

Practice 21: Review of Long O and the Sound /or/

1 Look at the picture and say the word. Then write the word.

_____ _____ _____ _____ _____ _____

2 Circle all the words that are the same as the first one.

note	not	note	tone	rote	note	vote	note
coal	coal	coat	coal	local	cool	coal	goal
short	snort	short	torn	sport	short	sort	shirt
flow	low	fowl	flow	flown	flaw	flow	slow

3 Make at least *8* words with these beginnings and endings:

b   one

m   old

sh ore

    ow

_____ _____

_____ _____

_____ _____

_____ _____

4 Use these words to fill in the blanks:

broke   cold   drove   home

goal   sport   roast   know

1. Joan served a pork _____ , corn, and hot rolls.

2. Do you _____ where to go to vote?

3. George tore his yellow _____ shirt when he wore it.

4. Tony and Rose Stone own their _____.

5. Did Joe catch a _____ after playing in the snow?

6. Rose _____ down the old dirt road.

7. They _____ into the store and stole some clothes.

8. I hope I will reach my _____.

Practice 22: Long a Words with Irregular Spellings

1 Read the words.

ea	**ear**	**ey**	**eigh**
break	bear	hey	eight
steak	pear	they	eighty
great	tear	prey	eighteen
	wear	obey	weigh
	swear		weight
ei		**ere**	sleigh
	eir		freight
veil		where	neighbor
vein	their	there	

2 Write the word you hear.

1. _____   10. _____   19. _____

2. _____   11. _____   20. _____

3. _____   12. _____   21. _____

4. _____   13. _____   22. _____

5. _____   14. _____   23. _____

6. _____   15. _____   24. _____

7. _____   16. _____   25. _____

8. _____   17. _____

9. _____   18. _____

3 Read the sentences.

1. My neighbor is gaining weight.

2. Grandmother is eighty years old.

3. Her great grandson is eighteen.

4. The bride is wearing a veil.

5. Hey, this steak tastes great!

6. Did the boys tear their shirts?

7. George did not obey orders.

8. Take the blood from a large vein.

9. Eight of us rode there in the sleigh.

10. He swears he will break out of jail.

11. They take their break at ten o'clock.

12. Where does that freight train go?

13. This chair has had years of wear and tear.

14. How much does that big bear weigh?

15. Our neighbors planted a pear tree.

16. Cats prey on mice and birds.

4 Homonyms: <u>there</u> and <u>their</u>

Set the box <u>there</u>.

Are <u>there</u> many letters?

They asked for <u>their</u> money back.

_____ were ten of us at the party.

We like _____ new home.

Sit down over _____ .

The children helped _____ parents.

Practice 23: Long e Words with Irregular Spellings

1 Read the words.

ie		i	ei
yield	chief	ski	weird
field	thief	police	seize
shield	brief	machine	either
niece	grief		neither
piece	belief		ceiling
priest	relief		deceive
shriek	believe		receive
pier	relieve		receipt

2 Write the word you hear.

1. _____   10. _____   19. _____
2. _____   11. _____   20. _____
3. _____   12. _____   21. _____
4. _____   13. _____   22. _____
5. _____   14. _____   23. _____
6. _____   15. _____   24. _____
7. _____   16. _____   25. _____
8. _____   17. _____   26. _____
9. _____   18. _____   27. _____

3 Read the sentences.   **Review word:** police

1. Does either of those machines work?

2. That priest has a firm belief in God.

3. The players ran out on the field.

4. We had no relief from the heat.

5. My niece gave a brief speech.

6. Joan hung a lamp from the ceiling.

7. Have a piece of cake.

8. A priest helped them in their grief.

9. I receive a receipt when I pay my rent.

10. Slow down as you come to a yield sign.

11. Neither Dave nor I know how to ski.

12. The chief of police seized the thief.

13. He carried a shield on his arm.

14. This shot will relieve your pain.

15. It's hard to believe he deceived us.

16. I heard a weird shriek from the pier.

4 Homonyms: <u>piece</u> and <u>peace</u>

Let's have <u>peace</u> and quiet!

After the war, there was <u>peace</u>.

She wrote on a <u>piece</u> of paper.

He played the piano <u>piece</u>.

Give me a _____ of toast.

The armies wanted _____ .

No one spoke. There was _____ .

The cup broke into _____ s.

Practice 24: Long O Words with Irregular Spellings

1 Read the words.

o	ew	oul
both	sew	soul
host	sewn	boulder
post		shoulder
ghost	**olk**	
most	folk	**ough**
almost	yolk	dough
		though
		although

2 Write the word you hear.

1. _____   10. _____
2. _____   11. _____
3. _____   12. _____
4. _____   13. _____
5. _____   14. _____
6. _____   15. _____
7. _____
8. _____
9. _____

3 Read the sentences.

1. The bread dough is rising.
2. Ghost stories scare me the most!
3. Add two yolks to the mix.
4. I carried the pack on my shoulders.
5. Rose sews most of her own clothes.
6. He felt sick. He went to work, though.
7. We both love folk dancing.
8. Fix the broken post on that fence.
9. Although we die, our souls live on.
10. Joan has sewn the seams on the skirt.
11. Both of us work at the post office.
12. The host thanked the guests for coming.
13. My folks know most of their neighbors.
14. A speed limit sign was posted.
15. A big boulder rolled down the hill.
16. Her hair is almost to her shoulders.

4 Homonyms: sew and so

The clothes you sew look so nice.

I'm tired, so I'll stop working.

I heard he left. Is that so?

That test was _____ hard!

_____ up the rip in this shirt.

What you say is just not _____ .

My car broke down, _____ I was late.

62

Practice 25: Irregular Spellings of the Sound /or/

1 Read the words.

w + ar	qu + ar	our	oor
war	quart	your	door
ward	quarter	pour	floor
warm	quarrel	four	
warn		fourth	
wart		court	
		course	
		source	
		mourn	

2 Write the word you hear.

1. _____   10. _____

2. _____   11. _____

3. _____   12. _____

4. _____   13. _____

5. _____   14. _____

6. _____   15. _____

7. _____   16. _____

8. _____   17. _____

9. _____   18. _____

---

3 Read the sentences.

1. He warned us that the floors were wet.

2. Please pour me a glass of milk.

3. There are four cups to a quart.

4. "Order in the court!" said the judge.

5. It's warm in here. Open the door.

6. Do you like your art courses?

7. Joe has warts on his hands.

8. We get news from many sources.

9. There is a warning sign on the door.

10. We mourn those who died in the war.

11. The nurses on the ward were quarreling.

12. He shot four holes on the golf course.

13. Is your office on the fourth floor?

14. A quart of pop sells for two quarters.

15. When did the team leave the court?

    After the fourth quarter, of course.

4 **Homonyms:** <u>war</u> and <u>wore</u>

Many soldiers fought in the <u>war</u>.

I <u>wore</u> that dress to the party.

We <u>wore</u> a hole in the rug.

She _____ that coat for years.

Did he die in the _____ ?

The army did not win the _____ .

He _____ out those shoes.

Practice 26: The Sound /e/ Spelled ea

1 Read the words.

ea

head	instead	death	health	breast
dead	steady	breath	healthy	
read	ready		wealth	weapon
lead		feather	wealthy	
bread	sweat	leather	jealous	meant
thread	sweater	weather		
spread	threat		heavy	
ahead		deaf	heaven	

2 Write the word you hear.

1. _____   10. _____   19. _____

2. _____   11. _____   20. _____

3. _____   12. _____   21. _____

4. _____   13. _____   22. _____

5. _____   14. _____   23. _____

6. _____   15. _____   24. _____

7. _____   16. _____   25. _____

8. _____   17. _____   26. _____

9. _____   18. _____   27. _____

3 Read the sentences.

1. Spread the jam on the bread.

2. The weapon was a heavy lead pipe.

3. She ran ahead of us at a steady pace.

4. He fell and hit his head. Is he dead?

5. As I spoke, the deaf man read my lips.

6. You sweat more in hot weather.

7. Stitch the seams with red thread.

8. Smoking is a threat to your health.

9. Joan will breast-feed her baby.

10. Rose is jealous of wealthy people.

11. The sweating runner stopped for breath.

12. The bird spread its tail feathers.

13. She is not ready to face death yet.

14. I meant to buy a leather coat.

   But I chose a heavy sweater instead.

15. You cannot take your wealth to heaven!

4 Homonyms: lead and led

My pencil lead broke.

Lead is a heavy metal.

He led the team to victory.

She led us down the hall.

That paint has _____ in it.

She _____ the class in singing.

The police _____ him away.

He works in a _____ mine.